WINE FOR GAME AND FISH

*The Sporting Wife's
Wine Companion*

WINE FOR

ILLUSTRATED WITH DRAWINGS BY BRIGID WITHERBY
AND REPRODUCTIONS OF 19TH CENTURY ENGRAVINGS

GAME AND FISH

The Sporting Wife's Wine Companion

By

JON HURLEY

H. F. & G. WITHERBY LTD

FIRST PUBLISHED 1986 BY
H. F. & G. WITHERBY LTD
32 AYLESBURY STREET
CLERKENWELL GREEN, LONDON EC1

PRINTED IN GREAT BRITAIN
BY BAS PRINTERS LIMITED
OVER WALLOP, HAMPSHIRE

CONTENTS

AUTHOR'S NOTE

Recent events in Austria have made one somewhat cautious about wholeheartedly recommending their wines, but it must be said the problem was largely with the dessert wines from Burgenland where a few unscrupulous and shadowy figures have endeavoured to make quality wines by methods other than the tried and tested formula of ripe grapes and dedication. A leading English shipper of Austrian wines has recently averred that less than one per cent of Austrian wines were thus treated, and he felt very sorry for the great majority of small and honest growers whose reputations have been dealt a blow from which it will take many free lunches and careful marketing before it recovers. The disturbing fact is that a few hitherto well respected names from Germany, Italy as well as Austria have been caught with their lederhosen decorating their ankles. My advice is to only buy wine from well established and reputable sources, and from merchants who deal directly with the growers and who can personally guarantee the wholesomeness of their suppliers' wines, and this is implicit in the recommendations and suggestions which I make throughout my book.

INTRODUCTION

Most readers of this book will readily agree that food, no matter how simple or exotic the recipe, is tremendously improved by the accompaniment of a bottle or two of wine.

Perhaps in an essentially non-wine making country like ours we do tend to make a bit of a fuss about complementing our menus with what we think are suitable wines. The French, who probably know more about wine and food than anyone in the world, take eating and drinking in their stride, and seem to enjoy the most peculiar combinations. It is not unusual for example to observe a Frenchman tucking into glasses of rich Sauternes with his soup, fish and meat courses, probably starting with the ultimate sacrilege, Port, as an aperitif!

There should be no strict rules about choosing wine and food but it is wiser not to open one's best bottles with dishes that are heavily spiced or containing ingredients hostile to the delicate flavours of the finer wines. The simpler the recipe the better chance good wine has to show its paces, and the best English meat, fish and vegetables provide the ideal backdrop for our finest bottles.

In writing a wine companion to Barbara Hargreaves widely read *The Sporting Wife – Game and Fish Cooking*, I have tried to make my suggestions for wines to accompany the recipes in this book both appropriate and interesting. I personally cannot see the point of drinking dull neutral wines, to be perfectly honest I would prefer good English cider or ale. Some of the wines I have chosen will not be readily to hand on our supermarket shelves but can be found at traditional wine merchants and specialists. Ask them for their lists and you will be drinking fine, personally selected wines, assembled by enthusiasts.

Our forefathers played a considerable part in helping to put Sherry, Port, Madeira and claret on the map, we drink more Champagne than anyone outside France, and although we are no longer the Port drinking champions of the world we do have the satisfaction of importing ninety percent of the best Port vintages. Our shops, off-licences, and, increasingly, our supermarkets, are brimming with good wines. Unlike our rather insular French, Italian and German friends, we have few local products to protect so we are among the luckiest wine drinkers in the world. However, it is important we use our wine merchants and show them we are still adventurous, and will not necessarily settle for branded products.

Some of my suggested wines are repeated under different recipes but wine is very adaptable and if, after studying the ingredients of each dish carefully, I have selected certain wines more than once it is because I have found the recipe to be complementary to the wine and vice versa. Besides, there is a finite range of good wines and this book will generally be consulted for just one recipe at a time, and is certainly not necessarily intended to be read right through in one sitting. My last chapter summarizes a large number of the wines mentioned, giving their type, price range and availability, and these are arranged in alphabetical order for easier reference.

Of course a great number of dishes contain ingredients sympathetic to several different types of wine which may in themselves conform to a certain general style. A rich dry white, for example, may be associated more readily with the creamy delights of good white Burgundy. Nowadays however the skill of the winemakers of Spain, California and Australia ensures that wines of similar if not identical style can be found in more than one country. So if the recipe demands a full bodied dry white wine it is worth remembering there is more than one supplier of this type of wine. Similarly, while claret is synonymous with Bordeaux, the essential ingredient which gives claret its distinctive taste and aroma is the Cabernet Sauvignon grape, and as this vine has been planted in almost all wine making countries, usually with some success, a Bordeaux style wine equally comes from Italy, Bulgaria, Chile or Yugoslavia, although one would not suggest with the same degree of finesse or balance as those giants from the Médoc.

Try new wines as often as possible, and remember no matter how good the wine you are currently drinking, a better bottle is just waiting to be discovered. My suggested lists of wine to accompany the recipes are not the Gospel engraved on stone tablets, but simply suggestions based on over twenty years of writing about, lecturing on, and more importantly, tasting the wonderful and multifarious wines of the world.

I hope that readers will find that some of the ideas in my book will add to the enjoyment of the recipes. There is much good wine to choose from, but naturally the choice is governed by the depth of one's purse. If some of my selections are out of reach, and the occasion doesn't warrant it, then one can always resort to a palatable *vin ordinaire* and still enjoy a lovely meal.

VINTAGE CHART

A short explanation of the chart is necessary.

The letters N.V. mean Non Vintage and they rarely if ever appear on a label, but a wine so described does not mean it is sub standard. On the contrary, many vintages produce wines of quite different and often compensating characteristics which when blended can produce quite an appealing and well balanced mixture which is far better than its original component parts. It always surprises me in fact to see very famous names putting vintages of quite execrable mediocrity on their illustrious labels when a judicious blend of these poor years would make a much better wine to be sold as non vintage. So we must hand it to the makers of Port and Champagne who only make vintage wines out of juice of exceptional quality. Occasionally, as in the Champagne vintage of 1978, a very small amount of quite good wine is made but in such minute quantities that it is generally unavailable to the average wine drinker, in such rare cases it is best to declare, as I have above, a Non Vintage year.

VINTAGE CHART

WINE	1970	1971	1972	1973	1974	1975	1976	1977	1978	1979	1980	1981	1982	1983	1984
CLARET	9	7	4	5	5	9	7	4	9	8	5	7	9	8	6
SAUTERNES	9	8	3	3	2	9	8	4	5	7	6	6	7	8	5
GRAVES (WHITE)	9	8	6	7	5	9	6	6	7	6	6	7	7	8	7
BURGUNDY (RED)	8	9	7	6	3	4	9	3	9	7	6	5	9	8	6
(WHITE)	8	9	6	8	6	6	8	5	8	7	6	6	9	8	6
RHONE	9	8	7	6	5	4	7	5	9	7	6	7	7	9	6
ALSACE	8	9	3	7	6	8	9	6	7	7	4	7	8	9	5
GERMAN	8	9	3	6	5	8	9	6	6	7	6	7	8	9	4
PIEDMONT	8	9	4	5	8	5	6	4	9	8	7	6	9	8	3
TUSCAN	8	9	4	5	7	8	5	7	8	8	7	7	9	8	3
CALIFORNIAN CABERNET SAUVIGNON	9	7	4	8	7	7	9	7	9	6	9	8	8	8	8
CALIFORNIAN CHARDONNAY	8	8	7	8	7	8	6	9	8	9	8	8	8	8	7
PORT	9	N.V.	3	N.V.	N.V.	6	N.V.	9	5	N.V.	7	N.V.	7	8	N.V.
CHAMPAGNE	7	8	N.V.	7	N.V.	9	8	N.V.	N.V.	7	N.V.	7	8	8	N.V.

9 Brilliant and exceptional, Reds need ten years, Whites at least three.
8 Very good, usually overshadowed by the really first class vintages.
7 Faster maturing bargains.
6 Modest and hopefully priced accordingly.
5 O.K. for punches and picnics.
4 Stick to the mineral water.

THE GRAPES

It is interesting to note that over half the finest wine grapes in the world are French. Good wine is, of course, made in many countries, and sometimes from grapes unknown outside their own areas. It is no accident, however, that certain countries whose previous efforts were confined to making imitation sherry and rough carafe wine have, since planting the finest French and German vines, been making a quality of wine once thought to be the sole prerogative of the finest European vineyards. It is difficult though to be precise about the exact part the grape plays in this scenario, but it is at least as important as the soil, climate, and skill and ambition of the grower. Here is a list of the most important grapes grown today in the vineyards of the world.

Black grapes

Brunello
One of Italy's important black grapes. Helps to make the expensive, respected and long lasting wine of Montalcino in Tuscany, but consult your vintage chart, there are disappointing years too.

Cabernet Franc
Makes fragrant wine in cooler areas and combines brilliantly with its more famous cousin, Cabernet Sauvignon. Responsible for adding a touch of freshness and perfume to the great red wines of Bordeaux, while on its own yields the delightful picnic wines of the Loire, including some of the best pink wine in France.

Cabernet Sauvignon
The greatest and most adaptable red wine grape on earth, capable of yielding good wine nearly everywhere; France, California, Australia, New Zealand, Chile, South Africa, Yugoslavia, Italy and Bulgaria. At the heart of the finest clarets, the best of which can be superb even after fifty years or more in bottle.

Gamay
The gentle but sprightly grape of Beaujolais is one of the most perfumed of red grapes, a veritable banker in blind tastings. Other countries have tried it but no-one can even get close to the delightful wine it produces on the granite hills of northern Beaujolais.

Grenache
Never brilliant on its own this strong sun-resistant grape helps to make tremendous wines in Châteauneuf-du-Pape and Rioja.

Merlot
This fine Pomerol and Saint-Emilion grape is an important contributor to the flavour and finesse of the great Médocs too. Quite capbable of producing wine of astounding quality, and surprising longevity when backed up with a judicious sprinkling of Cabernet Sauvignon. Château Petrus currently the most

fashionable and sought after red wine in the world contains no less than 95% Merlot. This soft gentle grape is now appearing with some success in California, Italy and Yugoslavia.

Nebbiolo
The tough, austere grape of Piedmont. Capable of longevity in Barolo, Barbaresco, Ghemme, Lessona and Gattinara and can reach heights of finesse and style if of a good vintage and coolly cellared.

Pinot Noir
Unlike the Cabernet Sauvignon, which sometimes needs other grapes to balance out its fierce tannin, the Pinot Noir on its own yields the most luscious Burgundies; bottles from the most elevated producers are now fetching higher prices than the greatest clarets but they lack the consistency and durability of the Bordeaux wines. The Pinot Noir is a poor traveller, quite incapable of making outstanding wine outside its native heath, except in Champagne where it is the principal grape, combining beautifully with Chardonnay its elegant Burgundian sister.

Sangiovese
A first cousin of Brunello, the fertile Sangiovese contributes something to most Tuscan blends but is chiefly known for that infuriatingly variable legend Chianti, which easily covers the red wine spectrum from horrid to magnificent. The name and reputation of the grower is all important here.

Syrah
Appears under various names in wine making countries where the sun shines as relentlessly as it does on the stony terraces of the Northern Rhône. Makes very drinkable wine even when young, soft and immature.

Tempranillo
A soft, gentle grape lacking acidity but essential in blends featuring tougher types. Plays an essential role in the finest Riojas and the emergent reds of Navarra.

White grapes

Chardonnay
The most important grape in the world for dry, full bodied white wine. At its best it yields wine of a creamy richness in Burgundy, California, Australia, New Zealand, parts of Spain and Italy, and also makes the delicate and delightful Blanc de Blanc Champagne, one of the tastiest of all sparkling wines.

Chenin Blanc
A versatile and much travelled grape capable of making a range of wines from bone dry Vouvrays to honeyed dessert wines on the banks of the Layon in the Loire Valley. It also contributes to Edelkeur, South Africa's most expensive dessert wine. California uses Chenin Blanc to make rich, dry wines, second only to Chardonnay in body and depth, if not in flavour.

Furmint
This grape nobly ripens like the Riesling, Semillon, Chenin Blanc and Gewürztraminer, and helps to make the famous Tokay Essencia, one of the great sweet wines. Harvested early it produces good sturdy off dry wines of modest quality.

Gewürztraminer
In Alsace it makes full bodied and spicy dry wines, not highly regarded by the general public but loved for half a century by the wine trade. Can also make strongly flavoured, if overpriced sweet wines too if the weather permits a late gathering of grapes. Californian versions can be good too.

13

Grüner Veltliner

A delightful grape which makes delicious wine in Austria and one feels it may also be quite capable of doing so elsewhere. A relatively new star with a pleasing personality.

Müller-Thurgau

This century old man-made cross between Sylvaner and Riesling vines has rather taken over in Germany and is now their most widely grown grape. Beloved of commercial wine merchants and growers, Müller-Thurgau wine is never great but is usually pleasantly drinkable and is very popular.

Muscat

The most widely planted sweet wine grape in the world, capable of making a wide range of scented wines from a bone dry version in Alsace to the rich dark maderised wines of Malaga and the south of France, also the ubiquitous but highly popular Asti Spumante. The nomadic Muscat also makes good sweet wines in Australia and California.

Palomino

Grown in pure chalk in Jerez, against the odds it makes surprisingly delicate Fino Sherry, the best and purest aperitif in the world.

Pinot Gris

This versatile grape has gradually assumed the mantle of workhorse of the European vineyards, and is known in many countries under such names as Rülander, Tokay, Tocai and Pinot Grigio. It makes solid wine of a fruity character and is dependable wherever it grows. So far only Alsace has enobled this doughty customer.

Riesling

Germany's greatest contribution to wine making. Makes wonderful wine ranging in style from the fresh green and scented Mosels to the fat, oily, golden rich Trockenbeerenausleses, among the finest sweet wines on earth. The Riesling travels quite well and makes good wine in the New World, though never up to the highest standards of the great Rheingau wines.

Sauvignon Blanc
At its finest in the best Sancerres, this deliciously sour grape makes wine of tartness with a flavour reminiscent of gooseberries. In hot conditions it can become flat, and coarse.

Semillon
A dull and neutral grape on its own but in Sauternes when the climate is right and the morning mists induce Botrytis cinera, Semillon is capable of making a wine that is the nearest thing to nectar this side of Paradise.

Viognier
This rarely seen grape struggles through the rocks and sand of the Northern Rhône to make fine expensive full bodied, long lasting, dry wine with an intriguing flowery bouquet.

Viura
An unheralded vine grown in Rioja which on its best form can make even the experts think of good, white Burgundy.

PREPARING WINE FOR THE TABLE
Wines are at their best when served at the correct temperature and that usually means cool, (but not deadened) for whites, rosés and light reds, and for finer, full reds the bottle must not feel either cold or warm to the touch. A half hour in the fridge or ice bucket is plenty for most wines meant to be served cool, while at least a day, or two if possible, standing on the sideboard will gently soften the big reds and allow any sediment to precipitate. Open light bodied wines just before you put them in the fridge, fine reds will benefit from an hour of breathing and then decanting if the quality and maturity warrants it. Never warm or chill wines quickly, whites will be stunned and reds will taste cooked.

CORKSCREWS

Use a simple classical corkscrew, (antique models are well made and not over-priced) with a thin, strong, sharply pointed spiral and pick the centre of the cork to penetrate until the tip of the screw appears in the bottle; then holding the bottle in a towel or teacloth to minimize injury in the event of a breakage, draw the cork gently. If the cork fragments don't worry, but it might be as well to decant and filter the wine.

DECANTING

Most red wine benefits from being taken out of the bottle where it may have been imprisoned with its protective chemicals for several years. This especially applies to the cheaper slightly sweet supermarket reds which, because of their residual sugar, are likely to re-ferment unless heavily dosed with sulphur dioxide. Strong beefy wines from Italy, Californians, South Africans and Australians are also improved by being exposed to a little fresh air.

Fine red wines and Port, even the better quality ruby Ports throw a sediment and it is obviously sensible to remove the wines from this. Decanting is easy and there is nothing magical about it. Tools required, apart from the sensible corkscrew described earlier, are a plastic funnel (a silver one will do), a six inch square of muslin and a decanter (those popular American litre jugs will do if nothing better is to hand). Remove the capsule and wipe away the dust and anti-cork weevil poison, and gently draw the cork (remember vintage Port and claret corks are longer, be sure to twist the corkscrew home. If the wine is very old the cork will almost certainly be crumbly and may fragment, but no need to panic, just get as much of the cork out of the bottle as possible then commence pouring. Once started, the pouring must be steady and continuous until the sediment starts to edge towards the mouth of the bottle. Experienced wine people can decant without the use of candles or torches but if in doubt place a torch (candles have been known to ignite the label or, worse still, burn the pourer's hand). Once the floating debris can be seen sailing towards the neck, stop pouring. It is better to waste meaningless and the French are probably the only major wine makers who persist in using such descriptions. *Tête de Cuvée*, *Réserve Speciale* and *Cuvée Réserve* are other adornments which suggest some sort of extra refinement or quality but are more often than not except in Alsace seen on perfectly ordinary wines.

(2) *Château Latour* is the name of the splendid house around which the grapes are grown before being made into wine on the premises. Châteaux of course come in many shapes and sizes and some are little more than countryside barns.

(3) *Premier Grand Cru Classé* means this particular estate's wine was plucked out of hundreds of clarets tasted and was placed joint first with three others in the 1855 classification. The reputation and selling price of the wines at that time were also taken into account. It means the piece of land upon which Château Latour stands is eternally sacrosanct regardless of the quality of the vintage, and only market forces and a thorough knowledge of the year will regulate the price this wine fetches.

GRAND VIN
DE
CHATEAU LATOUR
PREMIER GRAND CRU CLASSÉ
APPELLATION PAUILLAC CONTRÔLÉE
PAUILLAC-MÉDOC
1961
MIS EN BOUTEILLES AU CHÂTEAU

SOCIÉTÉ CIVILE DU VIGNOBLE DE CHÂTEAU LATOUR
PROPRIÉTAIRE A PAUILLAC-GIRONDE

In Germany on the other hand, every wine, regardless of the standing of the grower, has to earn its stripes each year by tasting and analytical tests.

(4) *Appellation Pauillac Controlée* confirms that this wine is a genuine example of the style and type made in the greatest, if not the prettiest wine village in France.

The Italians and Spaniards, belatedly, have their own versions called *Denominazione di Origine Controllata* (DOC) and *Denominacion de Origen* (DO) respectively, implying the approved grapes, methods of pruning, spraying and wine making conform to laws laborously evolved after decades of haggling. A few Italians have bucked the system by using French instead of Italian grapes and made the finest and most expensive plonks in the world.

(5) *Vintage 1961* In this instance the wine is fabulous, 1961 being one of the legendary vintages for claret. The year on the label refers to when the grapes were ripened, harvested and pressed into wine. As brilliance is impossible every year, check those vintage charts and you will find that quality or otherwise goes right through the range every time.

(6) *Mise en bouteilles au Château* usually indicates the wine was bottled at the same place where the wine was made and cellared. In Burgundy the phrase *Mise du Domaine* is commonly used while the Italians and Spaniards say *Imbottigliato all'origine* and *Embottellado en Bodega* followed by the name of the bottler. The Germans call it *Erzeugerabfüllung* but naughtily allow it on wines which sometimes have been made in great shiny gasometers by co-operatives.

Additional Information

Grape types are appearing more often now as are alcohol and bottle contents, which incidentally can vary by as much as seven centilitres per bottle. The term *Vin Délimité de Qualité Supérieure* (VDQS) denotes a lesser wine than AC, sometimes it is a sort of limbo where certain wines languish before the calling to full AC status. *Vin de Pays* is usually pleasant plonk while any word for table i.e. *Table*, *Tavola*, or *Tafel* means more or less the same thing, cheap and plentiful stuff which wine makers and their families gleefully dispose of in huge quantities. For

While a thread of similarity runs through the entire Teutonic range there are subtle differences to be observed. Mosel and Nahe wines share a common style, slate and silk, fruit and acid. The delicious acidity of the delectable produce of the Rheingau on the other hand is honed to a fine balance of sugar and grapey fullness that occurs nowhere else where the Riesling grape is grown. This unique quality makes the Hocks of the Rheingau the finest medium sweet wines on earth. Further south the land is flatter, the sun stronger, the grapes riper, the wine richer. The Palatinate is an area of fatter wines and the local wine contributes gloriously to this weight watcher's nightmare with its high glycerine and sugar content, wines to sip on verandas in the sinking sun of a beautiful day.

The better German wines keep surprisingly well and while a 1911 Gewürztraminer I once tasted was (not surprisingly) over the top, I have enjoyed plenty of twenty five year old bottles, especially those wiry creations from the stony vineyards of the Saar. German vintages to look out for include 1983, now being tipped as a "great", 1976 was also touted as one of the century's best but in retrospect the wines were too flabby (remember that sumptuous English summer?) and while the best are tenaciously holding on, a great many of the big names have turned a sickly yellow and prematurely expired. The 1971, also hailed as a giant, is at least living up to its reputation and a few bottles are still available, permitting those keen to sample an outstanding wine of the twentieth century, a taste of history, if you like.

reliable wine from elsewhere. Unlike the Cabernet Sauvignon which can make good wine almost anywhere, the Pinot Noir is a poor traveller and hardly ever shines in foreign parts. An exception being the German version, called Spätburgunder, which can be delightful if of a good vintage and the grower has allowed the sugar in the must to become alcohol. The Germans, often alas, prefer sweeter Pinot which is not to our taste.

France's third great area is the Rhône valley and here the wines are warm, sleepy and reliable. The northern Rhône is dominated by one grape, the silken Syrah, which while it improves greatly with keeping, even when grown by the more rustic, terribly dedicated growers, is soft and drinkable early. Further south on the flatter, rock strewn clay of Châteauneuf-du-Pape a veritable baker's dozen of different grapes clash and fight within the black uncouth liquid until tamed with age they become great wines but Clydesdales compared to the Derby winners of Bordeaux. There are however, plenty of value for money wines among the lesser known villages fighting to get their heads above the morass of big strong but dull reds from the sunny south of France.

There are other French wines, of course, and a good five or six years old Cru Beaujolais will sit down happily with a young Partridge, but the Gamay grape loses its charming freshness and edge with age and becomes more like an ordinary Pinot Noir. Good Beaujolais however is always keenly priced, and keeps quite well.

Nowadays there are many wonderful wines produced outside France. In the past decade or so the quality gap between the best wines of France and the best of Italy, Spain, California and Australia has narrowed.

Since the advent of their Denominazione di Origine Controllata (Italy's Appellation Controlée), their wines have proved a match for anyone, and while their main sales are still in the bulk end of the trade they also make large quantities of fine wines. Most of these are red and a few can be heartily recommended as partners to lightly hung game birds; six of the best reds in Italy hail from the Tuscany area. Most are to a greater or lesser extent made from the Sangiovese grape which makes wines less like Italian and more like French, and that is a compliment.

As an enthusiastic young entrant to the wine trade nearly twenty-five years ago I well remember the dulcet, onomatopoeic sweetness of the four Lombardy names Grumello, Sassella, Inferno and Valgella as they slid off the lecturer's tongue in the old Vintner's Hall in London as we studied for our trade examinations. Subsequent, and quite recent, tastings have alas confirmed the mellifluous quartet though sound enough, are not in the top echelon of even Italian red wines let alone in the minstrel's gallery of the great wines of the world. Labelled Valtellina Superiore the four mahogany coloured lightweights make an interesting comparison tasting and may then be enjoyed with cold game or a selection of good English cheeses.

Brunello di Montalcino is one of Italy's most expensive wines and in good years like 1970, 1975, 1977 and 1978 is worth every penny. Vino Nobile di Montelpulciano is another beautifully silky red and the best vintages correspond to those listed above. As in Bordeaux, there is a consistency of quality throughout the province in the better years. The long lasting Carmignano and the Tignanello have a few buckets of Cabernet Sauvignon in the blend which gives these wines an extra dimension. Like the Cabernet in Bordeaux, the brilliant Sangiovese is seldom used on its own and there is little doubt that a "cocktail" which includes a few other permitted types usually improves the wine.

Those red rivers of Chianti, much of it of dubious quality, that have gushed out of Tuscany for several centuries have not helped the reputation of this wine with its club-shaped bottle and, now, plastic raffia binding. It is worth remembering, however, that there are many great wines made in this large region. An estate-produced Classico riserva, sold in Bordeaux bottles, is quite a different proposition to much of the wine from the region found on the shelves of some cheaper stores. If wine drinkers are prepared to pay a little more they will instantly recognise the difference in quality.

Before leaving Tuscany there is another wine worth mentioning. Sassicaia is another tribute to the Cabernet Sauvignon, without a shadow of a doubt the best red wine grape on earth. This is a gorgeous wine with none of the "jammy-ness" associated with hot country Cabernet but it is expensive, and older bottles are very hard to find. Buy a bottle if you can, and stick it under the stairs for a year or two, you will find it a delight.

Piedmont, in northern Italy, is another quality wine area, but here the dominant grape is the Nebbiolo. The most famous name is Barolo but I personally have almost given up on this wine. I have tried dozens; cheap, frightfully dear, old, young, middle-aged, but the number of successes could be counted on two fingers. I prefer Barbaresco, Carema, Ghemme and Gattinara; they age well too. Mature Nebbiolo will compliment Partridge cooked to any of *The Sporting Wife's* recipes, and vintages to look for are 1970, 1971, 1974 and 1978.

Spain, too, has shown remarkable improvement in the past ten years and while the satiny oak-scented reds of Rioja are well established it is to the region of Catalonia we now look in admiration. Here a handful of skilful and sophisticated wine makers have surprised us with the sheer quality of their wines. I mention just two here, both from Penedès, not far from that famous haunt of sun seeking British tourists, Barcelona.

Miguel Torres experimented with non Spanish grapes in the Seventies and now his Gran Coronas Black Label is one of the greatest red wines in the world. Another Penedès grower recently to break through is American Jean León whose stylish Chardonnay is among the best. The enduring quality of the Cabernet Sauvignon shines through in Vega Sicilia, another amazing wine, this time from a desert as far as quality is concerned—Vallodolid. The classic Bordeaux mixture of Cabernet Sauvignon with a few Merlot, Malbec, and a little known Spanish grape, the Albillo, gives this luscious silky wine the class and style of a slightly roasted first growth claret. Aged for ten years in wood, an unheard of maturation time these days, Vega Sicilia after a further five years in bottle is still only coming round, a truly great red wine.

The fuller wines combining alcoholic strength, fruit and body are best matched with highly flavoured or richly sauced recipes. Here are a few ideas to go with Partridge which have been casseroled, braised or cooked with Sauerkraut, celery, apples or lots of herbs.

The fatter wines of Saint-Emilion and Pomerol and the thick Cabernets from California and Australia more than suffice. The velvety Syrah inspired wines of the northern Rhône, wines like

Côte Rôtie, Hermitage and St. Joseph will also suit as indeed would good Barolo or a Languedoc wine called Mas de Daumas Gassac. Made again from the Cabernet, which is organically grown, the latter should appeal to anyone worried about the amount of chemicals we are forced to take with our food and drink these days.

For Partridge pies, or served cold, spiced, puréed and even mildly curried, I would suggest good quality lower priced wines of interest to the enthusiast by virtue of unusual grape type, or method of production. There are plenty of these on our off-licence and supermarket shelves but we must forego the temptation to go for bulk at the expense of authenticity and character. For the Cabbage and Partridge soup I am sticking to fortified wine and as the little Mousses of Partridge are almost egg bound I am staying away from acidic northerly wines which, because of their lack of alcohol, tend to be fairly powerfully sulphured, particularly in bad years.

FOR YOUNG BIRDS; SPIT ROASTED; STEWED; BOILED; OR STUFFED AND OVEN ROASTED; AND SALMIS OF PARTRIDGE
Wines
Fine Bordeaux of good vintage and pedigree, fine old Rioja, mature Coronas Black Label, Sassicaia, Vega Sicilia, older Chianti Classico, (single estate if possible), mature Barbaresco, Gattinara, Ghemme, Carema, Brunello di Montalcino, Vino Nobile di Montelpulciano, Carmignano and Tignanello, fine mature Burgundy (Premier Cru or better), Cru Beaujolais, (Moulin-a-Vent with some bottle age), Château Musar (Lebanon), Cooks New Zealand Cabernet, Grange Hermitage (Australia's best red wine), Vranac from Yugoslavia.

FOR OLDER BIRDS; CASSEROLED; BRAISED; COOKED WITH APPLES; SAUERKRAUT; HERBS; CABBAGE; CHICORY; MUSHROOMS; OR SHERRY

Wines

Rich Cabernets from Australia, South Africa, California, Spain. Northern Rhône (Syrah based vines Côte Rôtie, St. Joseph, Cornas, Hermitage), Châteauneuf-du-Pape, Pomerol and Saint-Emilion, Barolo, Pinotage from South Africa, Shiraz from Australia, Zinfandel from California, Faros, Dingac, Postup from Yugoslavia, Bulgarian Mavrud.

PARTRIDGE PIE; COLD SPICED; A LA PURÉE; PAKISTAN SPICED

Chinon, young light Bordeaux, generic Burgundy, Beaujolais, modest Rhônes from Côtes du Ventoux, Vacqueyras or Lirac, reds from the Midi, Bergerac, Cahors, Côtes de Duras, Still red from Champagne, German Spätburgunder, Oregon Cabernet, inexpensive Italian reds—Chianti, Valpolicella, Bardolino, Cabernets, the soniferous Valgella, Sassella, Grumello and Inferno from Lombardy, (try Lambrusco from Emilia-Romagna chilled with the curry), Eastern European Bulls Blood, Bulgarian Cabernet, Yugoslavian Pinot Noir, Cabernet Sauvignon, or Cabernet Franc, young modern Rioja, cheap Californian varietals, Tavel and Provençal Rosés, Swiss Dôle, or a good Grecian red called Mavro Remeiko.

White wines

Gewürztraminer; mature German Spätlese, or Kabinett, Graves, Muscat d'Alsace, good vintage Sancerre or Pouilly Fumé, white Sauvignon wines from Bordeaux, dry Müller-Thurgau from Franken, or a popular Mosel from the middle.

LITTLE MOUSSES OF PARTRIDGE IN SHERRY SAUCE

Good quality dry Marsala, Fino, Manzanilla or Amontillado Sherry, medium Montilla, Sercial Madeira, older white Graves.

CABBAGE AND PARTRIDGE SOUP

Sercial Madeira, dry Montilla, Dry White Port, Château-Chalon, good nutty Amontillado Sherry, or old Malaga.

Wine with Quail

This delicately flavoured little bird is cooked in a variety of ways but often with apples, prunes, vine leaves, grapes and eggs, combinations not noted for their sympathy towards the elegant nuances of fine wine. Something assertive then is called for and there are a number of exciting possibilities in both red and white wines. The fresh acidity of northerly reds give those wines a brisk personality, allowing their grapey flavours to show. Old wine books suggest "Red Champagne" with Quail but these days one cannot take the great name in vain and the red wines of the Champagne region have to be called Coteaux Champenois. Gently chilled they are delightful, particularly if the weather is humid and the party flagging through over indulgence.

The most important red grape grown along the banks of the Loire is the Cabernet Franc, a less cultured cousin of the great Cabernet Sauvignon of Bordeaux. The Franc is pure of smell, fresh and light on the palate, and the taste lingers in the mouth. Taken on colour alone, a rawish purple, one would be tempted to stick it back in the rack for a few years; that, however, would be a mistake. The Cabernet Franc, like the Gamay of Beaujolais, loses its character with age and is at its peak after a year or two.

Placed in the usual order of seniority the Loire reds read Chinon, Saumur-Champigny and Saint-Nicolas-de-Bourgueil, but not long ago I tasted the wine of M. Pisani-Ferry, a young man who literally lives in a cave, a rather grand cave mind you. His wines are the best and most delicious Cabernet Franc I have tasted. Called Château de Targé, this small estate is worth a visit.

One of the better wines of Chinon is Le Colombier made by Yves Loiseau, a small grower at Beaumont-en-Veron, while visitors to the great old ruined Château de Chinon can see from the ramparts another good estate if they just cast their eyes down upon the gentle sloping vineyards of Clos de l'Echo which lies not a hundred metres from the battered and venerable old castle walls. The Saint-Nicolas-de-Bourgueil wines tend to be a fraction harder with less charm but they are excellent picnic wines for all that.

Beaujolais, the most gulpable red wine in France, is another delightful wine; and in spite of the tedious "Nouveau" race, good examples are freely available in the more thoughtful wine shops and supermarkets. Like most red wine it keeps quite well and does not, contrary to popular opinion, self destruct if not consumed within three weeks of finishing its fermentation. Old cobwebby bottles from the Twenties and Thirties occasionally turn up at wine auctions and they are a revelation. They may no longer be fresh but they compensate with smoothness and a mild, inoffensive maturity.

Rosé too can have a lot more character than one would think judging by the big selling brands, and robust Tavel from the arid Rhône is an important wine in its own right. It can be as good and meaty as many a red wine and bottles from the better vintages will actually throw a sediment when cellared. The gorgeous Gris Fumé, a frisky and flavoursome Loire wine, and the fairly expensive Château de Selle from the Côtes de Provence are also better than the average pink wines. The Cabernet Franc rosés too are interesting and, with their familiar Loire acidity, most refreshing.

Fragrant semi dry white wines from the purposeful Sauvignon, Gewürztraminer, Riesling, Muscat and Müller-Thurgau, as well as some of the new perfumed German crosses like Bacchus and Kerner, would add an extra dimension to any meal featuring quail. Traditionalists may still reach for their fine clarets and Burgundies but those with an inquiring mind and adventurous spirit may care to try one or two of the bottles listed below.

Red Wines
Coteaux Champenois, Chinon, Saint-Nicolas-de-Bourgueil, Saumur-Champigny, Irancy, Arbin, Chanturgues, Beaujolais, Passe-tout-grains, lesser Bordeaux from Fronsac, Bourg, Blaye, Cubzac, similar style light reds from Bergerac, Côtes-de-Buzet, Côtes-de-Duras, from Italy Dolcetto d'Alba, Grignolino and Vinòt, from Germany Trollinger, Spätburgunder, Austrian St. Laurent, Portuguese petillant reds from the Minho district.

White Wines
Riesling up to Kabinett quality from Germany, also from California, Australia and Northern Italy, Gewürztraminer from Alsace, Yugoslavia, Austria and Northern Italy, Zierfandler and Grüner Veltliner from Austria, Sauvignon Blanc from the Loire, (Sancerre and Pouilly-Fumé are best), Saint Bris, Bordeaux, and California, where it is known as Fumé Blanc, dry Muscat and Riesling from Alsace, Condrieu (a rare white Rhône but worth finding), Coteaux Champenois Blanc, Viña Esmeralda (a successful Spanish blend of Gewürztraminer and Muscat), English, if the product of a warm summer, Italian Verdicchio and Marino, Chacolí from Spain, Vinho Verde and Bucelas from Portugal, Zilavka and single estate whites from Northern Yugoslavia, Chardonnay from Bulgaria.

Rosés
Château de Selle, Rosé d'Anjou de Cabernet, German dry-ish Weissherbst, Gris Fumé, Tavel, try it at room temperature, and Marsannay from Northern Burgundy.

Serve Fine Wines with the following recipes:
ROAST PHEASANT, ROAST PHEASANT WITH MUSHROOMS, LINCOLNSHIRE RECIPE FOR PHEASANT, NORWEGIAN PHEASANT AND CUTLETS OF PHEASANT, AND FAISAN SAUTÉ AUX CHAMPIGNON

Recommended Wines
Fine mature claret, good vintages (try to memorise the best), Burgundy of Grand or Premier Cru status of the better years, and mature Rhônes. The fine wines from Piedmont. The Tuscan wines, Chianti Riservas (properties like Brolio and Badia a Coltibuono if possible), Brunello di Montalcino, Vino Nobile di Montelpulciano, Carmignano, Sassicaia and Tignanello, from Umbria Rubesco riserva, from Veneto, Venegazzu Della Casa and from the Basilicata the Aglianico del Vulture achieves style and verve with cellaring, while the other elegant Venetian wine, Castello di Roncade, is all too seldom seen on British tables. From Spain the Rioja Gran Reservas, the Penedès wine Gran Coronas Black Label from Bodegas Torres, and Vega Sicilia from Old Castile, Château Musar from the Lebanon is surprisingly good too.

Recommended Wines with:
PHEASANT PÂTÉ AND COUNTRY CAPTAIN
Beaujolais, Bardolino, Valpolicella, the gentle Caldaro and Cabernet wines from Trentino in Northern Italy, Chinon, St. Nicolas-de-Bourgueil, Saumur-Champigny, good dry German Spätburgunder, Trollinger, Portugieser, Limberger, and the Austrian Zweigelt and Blaufränkisch.

Whites:
Sauvignon, dry Chenin Blanc, Aligoté, Petit Chablis, Gewürztraminer, Alsation Muscat, Italian Pinot Grigio, Traminer Riesling, Soave Classico Superiore and Greco di Tufo, German wines of Kabinett quality, Hungarian Furmint, Badacsony and Kéknelyü, young white Rioja, sparkling white wines from France, Spain, Germany and Italy, the rosés from Provence, Tavel and Anjou.

Recipes
**PHEASANT PIE, STEWED PHEASANT WITH ONIONS,
FAISAN À LA CHOUCROUTE, PHEASANT WITH APPLES,
FAGIANO AL MADERA, PHEASANT À LA VIENNET,
PHEASANT WITH APPLE AND CALVADOS, PHEASANT À
LA GARFIELD, FAISAN AU VIN, PHEASANT PIE À LA
FRANÇAISE.**

Try: Cabernet Sauvignon varietals from California, Australia,
South Africa, New Zealand, Bulgaria, Penedès, Zinfandel from
California (the Concannon is excellent), Pinotage from South
Africa and Shiraz wines from Australia, California Pinot Noir,
the dark Mas de Daumas Gassac Cabernet Sauvignon from the
Languedoc, Barolo, and the dry Gutturnio dei Colli Piacentini
from Italy.

PHEASANT SOUP

Wines
Old Champagne, Sercial Madeira, Amontillado, Château-
Chalon, Tokay Szamorodni, Italian Vin Santo, Vernaccia di
Oristano, Spanish Cañamero, old fashioned Rueda, and
Yugoslavian Grk.

Wine with Grouse

This characteristic game bird of open moorlands is a clean feeder living off tender young shoots and seed-heads of heather and grasses on heath and moor in Scotland, Ireland, England and Wales. The birds vary in taste depending on the area in the British Isles they are reared, but on the whole they are stronger tasting than most other game birds, and usually considered to be one of the best of all. The pungency of the meat warrants imposing wine and I have made my selection with this in mind.

Because of its strong flavour grouse is delicious when eaten cold, and there are exciting wines to complement it when served this way.

It is possible to ring the changes with the various recipes and the fuller flavoured dishes, like the well hung "Sportsman's Grouse", need big, red wines to tone them down while the "Cold Terrine" and "Potted Grouse" are delicious with a salad tossed in olive oil, grated carrot, cucumber and a little homemade coleslaw and mayonnaise, and there are a number of outstandingly full bodied white wines to accompany them. Light red or white will go nicely with "Grouse Pie" while the "Grouse Soufflé" with its rice and eggs presents a bit of a poser but I have made a couple of suggestions.

Recipes
ROAST GROUSE, BROILED GROUSE WITH BACON

Wines
Château Musar, good St. Emilion and Pomerol, Barolo, Côte Rôtie, Hermitage and Châteauneuf-du-Pape, Cabernet from Jean Leon in Penedès and Cooks in New Zealand, Zinfandel; oaky Riojas, Taurasi from Italy and Portuguese Barca Velha.

Recipes
BRAISED GROUSE, SPORTSMAN'S GROUSE, GROUSE EN CASSEROLE, SALMIS OF GROUSE

Wines
Sunny Cabernets from California, South Africa, Australia and Spain, big young Riojas, Zinfandel, South African Pinotage, Australian Shiraz and Hermitage, Recioto Valpolicella, Californian Syrah, young Barolo, Mas de Daumas Gassac, Dão reds and Gutturnio dei Colli Piacentini from Italy, black Mavroudi from Delphi.

Recipes
COLD TERRINE OF GROUSE, TERRINE OF GROUSE, POTTED GROUSE

Wines
Gewürztraminer from Austria, Alsace and California,

Sauvignon Blanc from Bordeaux, Italy and California, Muscat from Alsace, Rieslings from Germany (up to Spätlese, older bottles are a little drier), Alsace, California and Australia. Chardonnay from the Maconnais and the Côte Chalonnaise, and same grape from Australia, New Zealand, California and Penedès. Italian Pinot Grigio and Cinqueterre, Zierfändler and Grüner Veltliner from Austria and Esmeralda from Penedès, Hungarian Ezerjó, Furmint Leanyka, Szürkebarát and Badacsony, Romanian Cotnari, Yugoslavian Traminer, Beli Pinot, Sauvignon and Riesling.

Recipes
GROUSE PIE AND GROUSE SOUFFLÉ

Wines
Crisp, light Loire style reds or assertive whites or rosés. Minor Bordeaux and Burgundies, VDQS reds and whites from the south of France, light Italian reds like Bardolino, Valpolicella, the cheaper Chiantis and Cabernets from northern Italy and Bulgaria.

Wine with Ptarmigan
This bird of the high mountains, unmistakable in its white plumage, is not great eating and is probably shot for the sport it offers. Perhaps because of its elusiveness there are very few recipes which depart from roasting simply in waistcoats of fatty bacon with butter for basting.

ROAST PTARMIGAN

Wines
The meatier Cabernets, Zinfandel, St. Emilion, Pomerol, Rhône, the Nebbiolo wines from Piedmont and the Brunello (or Sangiovese) wines of Tuscany. Hermitage, Shiraz from Australia and South Africa and the Italian Montelpulciano dei Molise.

Wine with Blackcock

A great favourite of Henry the Eighth, this bulky relative of the red grouse is good eating but not so fine to taste as his better known kinsman the grouse. The female is half the size of the cock and tastier.

Recipes

BLACKCOCK ROAST

Wines
Nice quality wines just outside the higher echelons of the Bordeaux Crus would suit admirably. There are lots to choose from among the Third, Fourth and Fifth Growths as well as good pickings in the thicket of Bourgeois wines. The best Italian Nebbiolos, Brunellos and rich "New Wave" Cabernets, and the Salice Salentino from Apulia.

Recipes
FILLETS OF BLACKCOCK FINANCIÈRE

Wines
This strongly flavoured recipe will require stronger wine, something to complement the rich sauce. The choice must be red with an alcoholic level on the high side for table wines, chunky Cabernets, Nebbiolo, Syrah, Shiraz, Hermitage or Pinotage would be ideal, also Châteauneuf-du-Pape and the Primitivo di Manduria, a hot black/red from Italy's heel and the basic Prokupac or the surprisingly tasty Vranac from Yugoslavia, the modest Castel Danielis from Greece or Othello from Cyprus.

Wine with Capercaillie
This huge bird, tasting of resin from feasting on pine needles, is obviously not one to warrant classic claret or Burgundy!

Recipes
ROASTED CAPERCAILLIE, ROASTED CAPERCAILLIE [YOUNG BIRDS]

Wines
Sturdy reds from sunny places with more alcohol than style, bags of fruit and the colour of blackcurrant juice. An alternative would be a cooled bone dry Sherry. At the turn of the century it was quite in order to drink Sherry throughout the meal, a far better idea than quaffing gassy Champagne. Try, too, the rich Sherry-like wines of Sardinia—Vernaccia di Oristano. Spain—Cañamero and the unusual Grk from the Yugoslavian island of Korcula.

Wine with Pigeon

The humble pigeon is one of the world's great survivors; shot at, trapped, netted, poisoned, it still multiplies, rearing its young on a crude platform of twigs in a windy bush or the ivy clad fork of a tree. Cooked with care, pigeon flesh is tender but spoils easily. It can still provide fare capable of testing the nuances of the finest wines, red or white.

Recipes
ROAST STUFFED PIGEON, POT ROAST PIGEON, PIGEON PIE, PIGEONS COOKED WITH GREEN PEAS, ROAST PIGEON

Wines
Red The finest bottles of red wine, mature claret, Burgundy, Rhône, Italian wines from Piedmont and Tuscany, silky old Rioja and the best of Penedès, and, of course, the great Vega Sicilia from Old Castile, also Barca Velha, a better than average Portuguese red, and the key Cabernets from Australia (Brand, Lake's Folly and Broken Wood are worth locating), the best Californians, and South Africans (Alto, Backsberg, Twee Jongegezellen, Rustenberg and Meerlust are names to seek).

White Mature Vouvray (Brédif, Huet, and Prince Poniatowsky are great names and their wines the cream of the crop, and yet never ridiculously expensive).

Recipes
JELLIED PIGEONS, TERRINE OF PIGEON, PIGEON PUDDING AND PIGEON PÂTÉ

Wines
Loire reds from the Cabernet Franc, light Bordeaux and Burgundies, Beaujolais, Bergerac, Côtes de Buzet, Cahors, Barbera, Grignolino, Dolcetto and Cabernet wines from Northern Italy, Bulgarian, New Zealand and Chilian Cabernets or any reasonable supermarket red (do read the labels, what is not on there is not in the bottle either).

on salt water, in which case the meat will smell fishy. Most cooks use oranges, vinegar, brandy, port, curacao, Marsala, juniper berries and lemon juice in their duck recipes so the wine list has to be tailored accordingly.

Recipes
ROAST DUCK [STANDARD RECIPE], SALAD, DUCK WITH SHARP SAUCE, DUCK WITH GIN AND ORANGE, ROAST TEAL IN ORANGE SAUCE

Wines
Big full flavoured Rieslings from Alsace, Germany, California and Australia, single estate Northern Yugoslavian, Gewürztraminer from Alsace and California, Yugoslavia, Italy, Muscat from Alsace, Rieslander, Morio-Muscat, Scheurebe, Kerner, Bacchus and Huxelrebe from England and Germany.

Recipes
SALMIS OF DUCK IN MARSALA SAUCE, CANARD SAUVAGE AUX BIGARADES

Wines
Honey sweet, late gathered Chenin Blanc from the Loire Valley. Moulin Touchais is gorgeous with an appropriate sweet/acid balance. Good quality Asti Spumante or old Malaga, well chilled is also worth a try, after all, the French have been known to serve Château d'Yquem with soup, lobster, duckling, steak, salad and dessert.

Recipes
ROAST MARINADE WILD DUCK, WILD DUCK IN BRANDY, CASSEROLED DUCK WITH SWEET PEPPERS, BRAISED WILD DUCK, WILD DUCK CASSEROLE, SALMIS DE CANARD SAUVAGE, BRAISED WILD DUCK FROM NEW ZEALAND, TEAL IN WYVERN'S WAY AND ROAST WIGEON

Wines
Strong reds from California, Australia or South Africa. They

are grapey, soft and agreeable but for downing rather than discussing. Cabernets, Zinfandels and Pinots and Syrahs, Shiraz and Hermitage from California and Australia. Estate Cabernets from South Africa, Vranac from Yugoslavia.

Recipes
ROAST TEAL [STANDARD RECIPE]

Wines
One duck dish worth perhaps broaching that revered bottle for. Fresh young Teal, simply served is kind to good claret, old Burgundy, mature Rhônes and Riojas, single estate Chianti Classico, other good Tuscan wines, and the fine Nebbiolos from Piedmont, and, perhaps less fine, but inexpensive, the ripest and best Portuguese, a mature Bairrada or Dão, Spanish Gran Coronas, the splendid Grange Hermitage, and the pick of the Californian Cabernets from the likes of Ridge, Heitz, Beaulieu, Mondavi and Mayacamas.

Wine with Goose
The wild goose is not the overweight and ambling watchdog of the farmyard, in fact it needs careful supervision during roasting if a charred carcase is to be avoided. So away with those scented, pleasantly acidic northern white wines and choose instead from your rack of reds. Roast Wild Goose will do justice to fine wine but older birds cooked in cider or wine will enjoy the company of good strong wines from sun-baked locations. Sensitive wine enthusiasts may, if they wish, forego the orange salad and apple sauce suggested in these recipes.

Recipes
ROAST WILD GOOSE

Wines
Fine French red wine from the classical areas, classified clarets and Premier and Grand Cru Burgundies. The best Italians from Tuscany and Piedmont. Mature Rioja and Cabernets from Penedès but I must again stress the need to consult a vintage chart, many of the great French names trade on the reputation of a few excellent years. There are many disappointing bottles.

Wine with Woodcock
This welcome visitor feeds on heather shoots, herbs and various insects. The meat is untainted and will not spoil the enjoyment of really good wine.

Recipes
ROAST WOODCOCK [SIMPLE RECIPE], BECCACCE AL SALMI

Wines
Fine red wine from the Bordeaux, Rhône and Burgundy areas, use the better bottles from the best vintages with ideally a minimum of ten years maturation in cask and bottle. The Médocs, Premier and Grand Cru Burgundies and the more serious wines from both the northern (softer Syrah based wines) and southern Rhône (heavier more muscular Châteauneuf-du-Pape), and the finest Italian and Spanish reds. Handpicked Californian, Australian or South African are often cheaper if not as elegantly muscular.

Recipes
STUFFED WOODCOCK [OLDER BIRDS], CREAMED WOODCOCK, WOODCOCK FLAMBÉE, ROAST WOODCOCK IN WHITE WINE

Wines
Good reds with a bit of character, the mature Chianti Classicos, well made Spanish, Bulgarian and Italian Cabernet, the lesser names from Saint Emilion, Pomerol, Fronsac, Blaye, Bourg and Graves, Cru Beaujolais and the generic Burgundies from good vintages, the cheaper and lighter American (try Oregon wine for a change) reds from both the Cabernet and Zinfandel grapes, and the Yugoslavian Vranac, Merlot and Pinot Noir based reds.

Recipes
WOODCOCK CONSOMMÉ

Wines
This rich concoction requires either the well known fortified accompaniment, or for a change, substantial Cabernet Sauvignon or Syrah wines from either good European vintages or the more consistent, if less exciting types, from southern climes. That finest of all white grapes, the dry Chardonnay, especially those with a whiff of oak from Burgundy, Penedès, Australia and California would also be most suitable. In Austria a dry Eiswein proved to be amazingly appropriate.

Wine with Snipe

Recipes
SNIPE PUDDING

Wines
Soft, medium sweet white wines, there are lots to choose from, slightly sweet Vouvray and Coteaux du Layon, white Saumur, warm vintage Alsace, German wines up to Spätlese quality, Abboccato Frascati, Orvieto, South African Late Harvest Chenin Blanc, Californian Chenin Blanc, Riesling and Gewürztraminer, New Zealand Chenin Blanc, wines from the

Recipes
SADDLE OF HARE IN CREAM SAUCE [OR IN GERMAN HASSENBRATEN MIT RAHMSAUCE]

Wines
German wine of Kabinett quality or Spätlese if either older or from the Saar where they seem to take on a little of the "cut" in the slatey soil.

Recipes
HARE IN SWEET SOUR SAUCE, MARINATED ROAST SADDLE OF HARE

Wine
Robust good quality reds from the traditionally heavy wine areas, Côte Rôtie, Hermitage, Saint Joseph, Cornas, Châteauneuf-du-Pape, southern Italy, Spain, California, Australia and South Africa.

Recipes
JUGGED HARE

Wine
Because of the sheer richness of this dish the ideal wine is a wiry and strongly flavoured red with little or no "baby fat", a sinewy Nebbiolo, Graves, Médoc or an oak aged and mahogany tinted Rioja, or one of those old woodworn Argentinians.

Recipes
HARE PÂTÉ RECIPES [1 AND 2]

Wines
Good quality but cheap reds and whites from your nearest supermarket shelf. Seek out what are the best and most interesting wines from the vast selection available. Spanish, Italian, Austrian and the Eastern European wines are good value and most are thoroughly reliable. Avoid the heavily blended brand names if you want to learn something of the variety of the worlds wines, and lose no opportunity to acquaint yourself with a new or unusual area or type of wine.

Recipes
PATE RECIPE [3]

Wines
With this altogether richer recipe the wine should be light, brisk
and fairly high in fruit acid. There are lots of sharp little thirst
quenchers which should admirably fit the bill. The Loire
Cabernets, Gamays and among the whites, Gros Plant,
Muscadet, dry Chenin Blanc and Sauvignon, the modern Entre-
Deux-Mers is sharper and inexpensive too. Don't overlook the
Vin De Pays and VDQS wines. Alsace provides suitable wines
too, particularly in less good years, and another area well worth
more than a cursory glance is Savoie. Here both Crépy and Seys-
sel are pleasantly different while their little travelled red called
Mondeuse is also worth finding. The crisp Sauvignon from Saint
Bris has been making waves in the wine busines for a few years
now while the tart Aligoté will cut through that fatty Pâté like
well honed Sheffield steel. For something a bit original try the
Oregon whites. The big oily Napa wines we know well but the
newish American versions are causing a few raised eyebrows,
can they be the answer to the American winemakers prayer for
more finesse and less beef?

Recipes
**HARE SOUP-BAWD BREE AND HARE SOUP [OLD
ANIMAL]**

Wines
Both of these very filling country broths need wine of character,
medium dry Montilla, real Sherry from Jerez, Vin Santo, Grk,
dry Tokay, Vin Jaune, Cañamero and Sercial Madeira will all
perform more than adequately.

Wine with Rabbit
Rabbit is a fairly neutral meat which cooks tend to make into
highly flavoured dishes swimming in rich winey sauces. But I
remember, admittedly perhaps through the rose (or perhaps the
rosé) tinted spectacles of nostalgia, my earlier days in the West
of Ireland running after horse drawn reapers. Then young rabbit

grilled over a turf fire and washed down with home made ale tasted like a food from the gods. For the purpose of this book we can examine each recipe and match the wines according to the strength and pungency of the added ingredients. The Italians in the province of Liguria do their rabbits in a sauce of red wine, tomato, garlic, rosemary and olives, not unlike our Rabbit in Marsala, and by merely substituting Chianti for Marsala we have more or less the same Mediterranean dish, which appropriately is served with good Italian vino.

Recipes
SAUTÉD RABBIT À LA CHARLTON, RABBIT IN MARSALA, RABBIT MARINADE, HARVEST RABBIT

Wines
Good red wine with backbone, clarets from outside the cherished 1855 divisions, (look again to the irony reds from Graves), mature Burgundies and Rhônes, mahogany tinted but elegant Italians. A wine from Liguria that especially goes so well with the dish described above—Rossese di Dolceacqua, which, while it might sound like "sweet water", in good years contains a strapping 13% of alcohol.

Recipes
MUSTARD RABBIT, LAPIN AUX PRUNEAUX, LAPIN AU CARAMEL, SAVOURY RABBIT GIBLETS, RABBIT PAPRIKA, FRIED RABBIT WITH TARTARE SAUCE

Wines
With these recipes I suggest strapping full bodied wines of character from the Californian, Australian and South African Syrah, Shiraz, Hermitage and Pinotage, the Italian Nebbiolo, Cabernet Sauvignon, Barbera and Cannonau, (from Sardinia). To go with the Rabbit Paprika, essentially an Hungarian speciality, we should try a Kadarka which is sold in great quantities over here as "Bull's Blood". The blood red bruisers made along the Dalmation coast in Yugoslavia i.e. Postup, would ably substitute too.

Recipes
SAUTED RABBIT À LA PAYSANNE WITH OLIVES

Wines
This recipe has an Iberian flavour and I suggest cool Sherry
or Montilla of medium body or one of the Sherry type table
wines such as wood aged white Rioja, Tokay Szamorodni or
those old yellowing relics usually from Burgundy or Graves
which often wind up friendless and worn out on the bargain
basements of the auctioneers lists.

Recipes
I don't agree that curry kills wine, it depends on the wine. Any
light chilled wine, red, white or rosé is a delightful companion
to a tasty curry and just to jog the memory there are plenty
from Northern France, those little vin de pays, minor appella-
tions, deliciously refreshing picnic wines of every hue. Try also
the peculiarly named Edelzwicker from Alsace, always cheap and
sound. The Gamay of Beaujolais and elsewhere is particularly
suitable in this context as are the Cabernets, both Sauvignon
and Franc, plus the "nouveau" style wines of Italy, i.e. the Piedmont trio of Primaticcio, Rubina di Cantavenna and the excellent Vinòt, an unusually light and crisp wine from that toughest
of good red grapes, the magnificent Nebbiolo. From the
Marches comes Falerio Del Colli Asolani. White wine drinkers
are equally well served in this light and bright department, our
supermarkets are bursting with little wines, experiment.

Recipes
RABBIT PIE AND TERRINE OF RABBIT

Wines
Nice well rounded reds will do here and there are a great number
from which to choose, chunky sun baked minor Rhônes or that
delightful claret-like wine from Provence, Château Vignelaure,
made without poisons or artificial aids of any kind. The old
Falernian wines were famous in Roman times and nowadays
they make gutsy reds called Falerno. Another good wine from

these parts is Fiorano made from the now classic blend of Cabernet Sauvignon and Merlot, while the ever reliable and still inexpensive Spanish Riojas are among the best value for money red wines in the world.

Wine with Venison
Venison, once a name applied to any kind of wild animal meat now refers only to the carcase of the deer, beautiful, timid creature which graces many of our woods and parks. Venison is increasing in popularity and with the advent of the ubiquitous freezer, haunches, fillets and loins are fairly accessible to the keen cook. The meat tends to be dry and sufficiently tough to warrant lengthy hanging and marinading. These practices may preclude the use of very fine and elegant wines.

Recipes
ROAST VENISON, ROAST HAUNCH

Wines
With a young animal, lightly hung, thinly sliced and served with simple English vegetables then good claret or Burgundy will not be wasted. Equally those excellent ripe wines of Italy, Spain and the Southern Hemisphere will add a dimension to the flesh of this majestic creature.

Recipes
MARINADED ROAST VENISON, TENDERLOIN STEAKS, VENISON STEWED IN BEER, SPICED VENISON

Wines
Bigger wines are required here, fruity, alcoholic ones from the Rhône Valley, the good beefy reds from the Languedoc, the massive Amarone, the potently elegant Torrette from Veneto, Santa Maddalena from Trentino—Alto Adige, Schioppettino and Refosco from Friuli-Venezia Giulia and Rossese di Dolceacqua from Liguria. Also the good soft dark wines of Penedès, Nevarra and Priorato, and the "jammy" workaday reds from South Africa, Australia and California.

Recipes
LEG AND LOIN OF VENISON IN CREAM SAUCE
[REHBRATEN MIT RAHMSAUCE]

Wines
A German red would go nicely with this but they are a bit scarce. If unable to locate a Limburger, Trollinger, Müllerebe or Spätburgunder then select an equivalent from elsewhere—the Austrian Saint Laurent and Blaufränkisch (the Beaujolais Gamay well disguised).

Recipes
VENISON MEAT LOAF, DEER HAGGIS

Wines
Poorer cousins of claret will do—Bergerac, Côtes de Buzet, Cahors, Côtes du Marmandais, Côtes de Duras, the lightweight Italians, e.g. Valpolicella and Bardolino, and Bulgarian and Chilian Cabernet Sauvignons.

Recipes
VENISON LIVER PÂTÉ

Wines
If taken as a picnic or luncheon snack the wines above will suffice. If, however, the pâté is to be served as an hors d'oeuvre then dry Sercial, Montilla or Fino Sherry would be more in keeping, and would lead nicely into whatever wines may follow.

Recipes
VENISON GOULASH

Wines
Although I am instinctively against any form of standardisation in wine the Hungarian wine most commonly seen in the U.K. is the blended and cleverly marketed Bull's Blood. Made from a mixture of Kadarka, Merlot and Cabernet Sauvignon grapes it has the virtue of being sound and widely distributed. The Pinot Noir and Gamay grapes known respectively as

Nágyburgundi and Kékfrankos also make good wine in Hungary and are worth inquiring after. Hungary, like its neighbour Yugoslavia, is warm and fertile and makes far better wines than the few we normally come by in our supermarkets and off licences.

Recipes
GAME SOUP

Wines
Either the white wine being served with the first courses or medium Montilla, Amontillado or Palo Cortado Sherry, Sercial Madeira, dry white Port, or any of the oxidised white wines mentioned earlier.

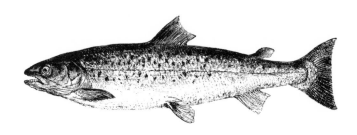

Wine with Salmon

The adventurous and widely travelled salmon brings delight to fishermen and gastronomes throughout the world. A young hen fish hooked early in the season makes superb eating and so varied are the ways of cooking these beautiful and mysterious creatures that many types of wine may be used successfully to accompany a wide range of salmon recipes.

Recipes
POACHED SALMON [WHOLE FISH], POACHED SALMON [STEAKS AND CUTS], BAKED SALMON

Wines
The fullest whites in the cellar will go nicely with this selection of fairly plain but excellent recipes. All the great Côte de Beaune white wines—the Montrachets, Meursaults, and sumptious Cortons, as well as the Grand Crus from further north in Chablis. But Chardonnay wines of great quality are no longer confined to that tiny part of France and we can look with absolute confidence to Penedès in Spain, where Jean Leon makes a creamy, full bodied wine with more than a hint of oak. In California too there are several growers large and small turning out barrels of gleaming golden Chardonnay, full of flavour, body and alcohol. The Australians too have broken through the quality barrier, as indeed have their neighbours, New Zealand. Prices across this glorious Chardonnay spectrum range from cheap mass produced but excellent American wine to the magical but fearfully expensive Montrachet. The latter classic, however, needs a great vintage to justify its price while the

opposition from warmer places seems to be able to achieve acceptable standards nearly every year.

Recipes
GRILLED SALMON VERMOUTH, BAKED SALMON NEW ORLEANS, KIPPERED SALMON

Wines
While neither of these dishes would frighten a big imposing oaky Napa Valley Chardonnay they might destroy the more delicate nuances of a good Chablis or the lighter Côte de Beaunes. Muscular white Hermitage, white Châteauneuf-du-Pape or a Graves such as Olivier, Chevalier or Laville-Haut-Brion, or, from Italy, the lovely but inconsistent Clastidium, or Greco di Tufo or the Spanish silky, smooth, oak scented Rioja Ygay, might be more appropriate. The less pecunious could of course settle for a good Macon (ordinary Pouilly-Fuissé is hackneyed, but the few single domaines are good) and Saint Véran, quite recently elevated to Appellation Controlée, is reliable.

Recipes
SALMON PÂTÉ, SALMON MOUSSE, SALMON CUTLETS À LA BERGEN, SLICES OF SALMON SUEDOISE

Wines
Butter and cream play no small part in the preparation of these recipes so it might be prudent to go north for our wines where the grapes are greener and the acidity higher. The less fragrant Alsation wines (house blends featuring second eleven grapes), Muscadet, Gros Plant, dry Vouvray, Montlouis, Savennières, Jasnières, Quincy, Sancerre and Pouilly-Fumé, and the thin Aligoté from Burgundy are available now in our supermarkets and wine shops. These are crisp, sharp, refreshing wines capable of handling those cream laden concoctions. German and Austrian Trocken wines would also suit, as indeed would Luxembourg or English wines. Rosé or red from these areas may also be tried if one is feeling particularly adventurous.

Recipes
**HOT SALMON SOUFFLÉ, SALMON ROE [AS A
SUBSTITUTE FOR CAVIAR]**

Wines
This eggy soufflé might benefit from the steadying influence of
a good, nicely chilled Montilla or bone dry Fino or Manzanilla.

Recipes
SALMON ROES [AS A SUBSTITUTE FOR CAVIAR]

Wines
One could take the pretence all the way and knock back a few
quick Vodkas with our imitation caviar, or more sensibly
perhaps take it with a nice clear, fruity sparkler from the Loire.
Italian, and Spanish, Méthode Champenoise wines are first rate.
Champagne, of course, when it's good, is unbeatable, when it
isn't, then two bottles of the other type would be infinitely better
value.

Wine with Sea Trout

In his introduction to *The Sporting Wife's* chapter on Sea Trout,
Hugh Falkus paints an evocative and poetic cameo of the quiet
joys of an angler hooking his quarry in the stillness of the evening
then fighting to land it as darkness descends. All the more
important therefore when faced with this noble protagonist
stretched out appetisingly on the plate that a fine wine should
be selected. Many Salmon and Sea Trout recipes are inter-
changeable and the wines selected for the Salmon dishes may
be used successfully with Sea Trout. Here, however, are a few
alternatives.

Recipes
JELLIED SEA TROUT, SEA TROUT CUSSY

Wines
An elegant and fragrant wine is suggested here, something clean
and sharp with the touch of class a single estate's care and atten-
tion to detail engenders. Sancerre with its delightful tang, with
the added weight of a good summer behind it, is always
appropriate. While those craving a soupçon of sweetness may
plump instead for a lightly-scented Riesling of Kabinett quality
from the Rheingau, or one of those slate sharp green wines of
the Saar.

Recipes
SEA TROUT IN RED WINE

Wines
The idea that one shouldn't drink red wine with fish is of course
nonsense and with this recipe with its cream, flour and herbs
I am going for a Grand Cru Beaujolais of a recent good vintage.
Here the perfumed Gamay grape with a little richness and a
touch extra alcohol decreed by its status, should provide an
interesting partner.

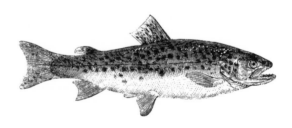

Wine with Trout
While so much of what the modern town dwelling fisherman
catches is for the sport he is probably happiest when returning
home with something edible, and there are few greater pleasures
than sitting on a shady bank above a quiet, well stocked pool

anticipating a tasty supper of grilled trout, wholemeal bread, and a beaded carafe of cool crisply dry wine. Trout and sea trout make delicious eating and can tax the ingenuity of the cook, such is the great variety of ways they can be served. Boiling in white wine is a popular way and is something worth saving those wine dregs for.

Recipes
RIVER AND RESERVOIR TROUT

Wines
The subtle taste of trout can be enhanced by a light wine with a pleasant fragrance. Any of the German wines will suit, especially the Riesling or Riesling derivatives like Müller-Thurgau, Kerner or Bacchus. Wines up to Kabinett quality with a fruit acid balance are best. The Italians living in the province of Molise which has the Adriatic lapping its doorstep eat plenty of trout with their Ramitello Bianco. We may have to make do with the more often seen Frascati or Soave, both of which feature the Trebbiano grape. With the Alpine Blue trout of Trentino—Alto Adige, the recommended wine is the locally produced Müller-Thurgau. The Germans, too, love their trout and a common sight on tables in the restaurants fronting the Mosel is the famous Blau Forelle, lightly cooked and served, of course, with the delicious, scented wines grown high above the majestic river. Alsation Riesling, Muscat or Gewürztraminer, French Sauvignon Blanc, Italian Vin du Conseil, or Blanc de Morgex, Riesling Renano, Traminer, Verdicchio and Verduzzo Ramandolo, Oregon Riesling and Sauvignon Blanc, South African Steen, Australian Clare-Watervale Riesling will also fit the bill.

Recipes
THE IRISH GHILLIES' WAY OF BAKING TROUT

Wines
This must be one of the most romantic recipes of all, but pioneers must remember to take along the Sunday papers, for an essential part of the recipe involves wrapping the trout in wet newspapers and burying them in the hot ashes of the camp fire.

It may surprise the old enemy to learn there are vineyards in Ireland, several of them, along the south coast and they say the wine, (I have yet to taste a bottle), is twice as good as the English stuff. But they would, wouldn't they? The grapes used are the same as in England, Müller-Thurgau mainly, and some summers are sufficiently warm to warrant only a small amount of chaptalizing—the addition of sugar at vintage time. Make do with a clean tasting Richensteiner Seyval Blanc or Müller-Thurgau from the neatly cultivated back garden vineyards of the Home Counties.

Recipes
OTAK-OTAK, BOILED TROUT, HELL FIRE TROUT

Wines
These recipes contain spices, coriander, garlic, red peppers and so on; so a wine with a bit of weight is called for. Petit Chablis, Côte Chalonnaise (Montagny Premier Crus) or Maconnais (plus village name, i.e. Lugny), Sylvaner from Alsace or Germany, Frascati, Soave, Torre di Giano, Lugana, Ramitello, Donna Marzia and Furmentin from Italy, Rioja Blanco, Viña Sol and Marfil from Spain, and Dão and Bucelas from Portugal.

Recipes
TRUITES AU LARD

Wines
Any light wine with a fair amount of fruit acid, English, Muscadet, Gros Plant, Sauvignon, Riesling, Aligoté or any Chardonnay of moderate quality will do with this slightly greasy dish. If red is the choice then go for Loire, German, Austrian and Northern Italian.

Recipes
TRUITES AU BLEU

Wines
If the cook goes easy on the vinegar stipulated in the recipe then this classic German dish demands the elegant, fruity and delicate wines of the great river Mosel. Our shops and supermarkets are well stocked with them, to be on the safe side choose a well-known name of Kabinett quality.

Recipe from The Compleat Angler
The legendary author and fisherman, Isaac Walton, came up with a novel way to cook trout. The recipe featured among other things stale beer, vinegar, white wine, rind of lemon, horse radish root and a "handsome little faggot of rosemary, thyme and winter savoury". Of course one may drink anything with his dish (as indeed one can with any recipe), but how about a good Real Ale, something like Wadsworth 6X or Hook Norton's Best?

Wine with Char
This red-breasted fellow was even mentioned by Saint Evremond in one of his epistles or so the story goes, whatever the truth of it the saffron fleshed creature makes tasty eating.

Recipes
CHAR À LA CRÈME

Wines
Fetch out the better white Burgundies, fine Grand or Premier Cru Chablis, Meursault, Montrachet of important vintages, or the better single domaine wines from elsewhere in the region. If going "foreign" then choose the best Californian Chardonnays from the boutique wineries, Chalone, Château Montelena, Château St. Jean, Dry Creek, Freemark Abbey or Joe Heitz. Also the fine Petaluma and Saxonvale versions from Australia and one of Italy's best white wines made in the Emilia Romagna region on the Terre Rosse estate. Chardonnay, greatest of all dry white wine grapes, has the Cabernet Sauvignon's (its red

compatriot), penchant for making successful wine almost everywhere it is planted.

Recipes
POTTED CHAR

Wines
Delicious cold fragrant wine with a rich, flowery bouquet and some style is called for. Most of the multitude of new grape types pouring out of the German viticultural research stations would make gorgeously appropriate wines. On the other hand it might be an opportune moment to crack a good bottle of fizz. A few amazing bottles stand out among the vats of acidic sparklers and not surprisingly they come from Reims or Epernay. My favourites are Krug Private Cuvée, Pèrrier-Jouet's Belle Epoque, Roederer's Cristal Brut and the brilliantly elegant Comtes de Champagne from the house of Taittinger.

Wine with Pike

This tyrant of a fish which "devoureth not only other fishes but his own kind as well" is difficult to prepare and wasteful too, as less than an eighth of his weight is good boneless meat. What is left, however, is tasty enough—witness this remark by Rev. Batchelor, "as pheasant is to chicken", he intoned, "so pike is to cod". Pike dishes can handle big wine, rich, honeyed Chardonnays from warm vineyards, handsome white Rhônes, Domaine du Vieux Télégraphe is lovely, or tough Gran Viña Sol from Penedès.

Recipes
PIKE WITH HORSERADISH SAUCE, PIKE WITH WHITE WINE, BAKED PIKE

Wines
Chardonnays from the Côte de Beaune, California, Australia and Penedès. Gran Viña Sol from Penedès, Ygrec or similar quality oaky Rioja of some age, Elba Bianco, Gavi dei Gavi, Greco di Tufo, Marègia, Villa Antinori Bianco, Soave Classico Superiore, Frascati Superiore from Italy, or classed growth white Graves, Rhône whites, German Trockens of good vintage from Franken and Baden.

Wine with Carp
A sprightly, fairly full-bodied wine is needed to bring carp to life as he is not the most exciting member of the fish family. With Blue Carp, a simple classic dish, decent Riesling or Gewürztraminer would be admirable, but strongly flavoured recipes warrant more muscular wine.

Recipes
BLUE CARP

Wines
Gewürztraminer from the usual sources—Alsace, Italy, (this grape's home town is said to be Tramin in Trentino-Alto Adige and the wine called Traminer Aromatico is worth getting hold of), Austria, Yugoslavia, Germany, California and Oregon. Rieslings from around the world and the elegantly dry Muscat of Alsace would be able substitutes.

Recipes
DELICIOUS CARP, GINGERBREAD CARP, COMPLEAT ANGLER RECIPE, CARP A LA RUSSE

Wines
Dry Austrian wines (from the untainted North) are certainly well worth considering, they are a fraction fuller than their

Teutonic neighbours but their quality is undeniable and they are inexpensive. A strongly scented Spanish wine called Esmeralda from the Torres estate is a fairly recent success and if innovators ought to be encouraged then also look at the good Chenin Blan from Cooks in New Zealand, and the Wooton Müller-Thurgaus of our own Major Gillespie.

Wine with Perch
This wholesome fish is revered by gastronomes everywhere and its delicate flesh combines beautifully with fine wine. These mainly French recipes deserve the best white wines from that greatest of all wine making countries.

Recipes
**PERCH IN WHITE WINE, PERCH À LA BELENNE,
BEIGNETS DE PERCHE DE TANTE MARIA DUBORGEL,
PERCHE SOUCHÉ**

Wines
Fine Chablis Grand or Premier Cru of a good vintage, the meatier white Beaunes, Château-Grillet, that stunningly fragrant and expensive white Rhone wine made from the rare Viognier grape, estate bottled Sancerre and that splendid big, dry Chenin Blanc made in Madame Joly's lovely old walled vineyard, Coulée de Serrant near Savennières on the Loire, this brilliant wine is available through the best traditional wine merchants.

Wine with Bream
The Bream burrows deep into the muddy beds of rivers when he spots a pike stealing up astern, thereby spoiling a good lunch. A delicate tasting fish, Bream will not disgrace good wine and cooked simply in a little white wine, butter and shallots will harmonise perfectly with the more perfumed wines of the world.

Recipes
STUFFED BREAM, BAKED BREAM

Wines
Choose authoritative white wine with alcohol and body, sunny Chardonnays, large dry Chenins, decent Château bottled

Graves, oaky Rioja and the golden dry wines of Italy, Australia and California.

Recipes
BRÊME À LA MODE DU PECHEUR

Wines
This plain dish will suit really good white wine from the cooler areas. Authentic Saar wine is beautifully fresh, fragrant and above average, and wines to look out for are the handmade gems from the estates of Edmund Reverchon at Konz and Egon Muller at Wiltingen.

Wine with Tench
This near relative of the carp is a strange character with, according to Mr. Walton, the healer's touch and it can cure the feared pike with the flick of a fin. In fact, Tench has such power over the pike that the latter "forbears to devour him though he be never so hungry". Well, we have no such qualms and Tench cooked French style in white wine makes a tasty meal.

Recipes
TENCH À LA POULETTE, STUFFED TENCH

Wines
Still white wine from the hills around Champagne, Chablis, or the good but affordable Chardonnay wines from the better villages in the Maconnais.

Wine with Barbel
This very powerful fish is yet another distant member of the carp family but is not favoured by gourmands, due to its profusion of spiky bones.

Wines
Good, dry whites from any of the classic regions of France may wash it down nicely, but so will the wines of character from the most unlikely places. Take another look at the inexpensive and fruity Germanic style wines from the Eastern Bloc countries.

Wine with Grayling

Recipes
BUTTERED GRAYLING

Wines
This fish spawns later than its cousin the trout, and is at its best for eating in the late autumn. Its aroma of water thyme lends itself to an appley Muscadet Sur Lie, or the delicate whites of Italy—young Blanc de Morgex, Blanc de Cossan, and Blanc de la Salle all produced high up in Valle di Aosta Italy's smallest and most northerly region, or any one of the almondy delights produced the length and breadth of that fecund, wine soaked land.

Wine with Eels
This extraordinary creature abounds in our British rivers and streams and is very good to eat either fried, jellied, or in a sort of loaf the way the Severn fishermen cook them. Eels are among the very few fish that cause red wine to spring more immediately to mind than white. The Italians too like eels and they have an Umbrian dish called Anguille alle brace—grilled eels from the Lake Trasimeno which they serve with the local red wine made from both Italian and French grapes.

Wines
Delicious quaffing bluey/pink reds from Alsace (here the Pinot makes an interesting sharp wine), the regular Loire Cabernet Franc trio, plus any European wines made from the Gamay, i.e. Beaujolais, or Saint Pourçain, Arbin, Chanturges, German and Austrian reds, Italian Valpolicella, Lambrusco, (try the white version, quite palatable), Bardolino, Ischia, Tuscany's "Beaujolais Nouveau" called Nuovo Fiore, the list is long. Try also the "green" reds of the Minho in northern Portugal.

Recipes
JELLIED EELS

Wines
Any white or red dry wine will suit this but the most ethnic way to eat jellied eels is on a balmy summer's evening clutching a pint of Red Barrel, wearing a funny hat, and within sight and sound of Southend Pier.

Wine with Sole

Sole is sold in many restaurants with the prefix Lemon, which distinguishes it from Dover Sole, that most succulent of flatfish and adored the world over by gourmands and gastronomes. Dover Sole is to Lemon Sole what Californian Chablis is to the famous French wine, and when merely fried in egg and bread-crumbs is the partner par excellence for characterful dry white wine, medium bodied white Burgundy and estate bottled Sancerre of a ripe vintage, or a Vouvray sec from one of the traditionally fine producers like Marc Brédif or Domaine des Bideaudières.

Recipes
FRIED SOLE, SOLE DUGLÉRÉ

Wines
First rate Sancerre, Vouvray or Chablis, Italian Torre di Giano, Trentino Chardonnay, Austrian Grüner Veltliner, Oregon Chardonnay, dryish German Kabinetts.

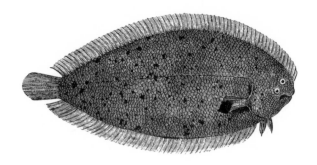

Recipes
**FILLETS OF SOLE FLORENTINE, FILLETS OF SOLE
BONNE FEMME, SOLE À LA BON HOMME**

Wines
The ingredients used in these recipes are more suited to bigger
wines, the sunny, glycerine coated golden whites of the better
sited vineyards in Burgundy, Italy, Spain and the New World.
Premier and Grand Cru Burgundies, Château Grillet, Chardon-
nays from the noted new producers in Spain, Italy, Australia
and California, Italian Gavi dei Gavi, Donna Marzia, Favonio,
Montecarlo and Vernaccia di San Gimignano, the Spanish Gran
Viña Sol, Condrieu and the chunky Hermitage Blanc from the
Côtes-du-Rhône.

Wine with Plaice

Recipes
PLAICE, FRIED AND STUFFED

Wines
The Chenin trio, Saumur Blanc, Vouvray, and Montlouis,
young fruity Alsatian Riesling, Gewürztraminer, or Muscat,
good village Macon, the lesser known but excellent dry German
wines from Franken and Baden. Californian mass produced
varietals (they are good value for money), and anything interesting from Italy or Australia you haven't already tried.

Wine with Flounder

Recipes
FRIED FILLETS OF FLOUNDER

Wines
Any crisp fragrant dry white, the tastiest and most fragrant tend
to come from the cooler areas of the world's wine map, Northern
France, Germany, Northern Italy, although modern methods
of vinification are starting to blur those once handy
generalisations.

Recipes
SWEDISH ROLLED FILLETS WITH LEMON SAUCE

Wines
The lemon with its sour acidity will taste better with a wine
lacking in that department so go for the warmer wines, there
is plenty of reliable, if dull, dry white Bordeaux about, (a decade
or so ago the popular taste for dull sweet wine was from the
Côtes de Bordeaux, Graves de Vayres and Entre-Deux-Mers,
unashamedly piped all from the same vat), also anything made
from the Sylvaner and Semillon grapes.

Wine with Dab
As they are cooked in similar ways to Flounder the same wines
will apply but be adventurous, try something not listed.

Recipes
DAB WITH ROE STUFFING

Wines
Any decent dry or medium dry white of recent vintage (the
cheaper range tend not to have much of a shelf life so buy the
youngest).

Wine with Turbot
This big sea fish makes surprisingly tasty eating and warrants
a decent wine of some weight.

Wines
Coulée de Serrant, Grand Cru Chablis and Beaunes, fine Rioja blanco, Gavi dei Gavi, the best Penedès, Australian, New Zealand Chardonnays, and Californian Chardonnay from the wineries of Joe Heitz, Chalone, Château Montelena, Zaca Mesa and Trefethen.

Wine with Halibut
This, the largest of flatfish, lives in the deep waters of the Northern Seas and when caught is often frozen which takes away much of the delicate flavour of the fish. Thus the cook's expertise is needed to impart some flavour, and a wine of character is therefore required.

Recipes
CHICKEN HALIBUT WITH CHEESE SAUCE, BAKED HALIBUT

Wines
Strong, full-bodied Rieslings, Gewürztraminers of good Alsation vintages, the best Californians, especially Simi, Château St. Jean, Freemark Abbey, Grgich-Hills Cellars, Jekel Vineyards, any Joe Phelps, also, though not in the same league yet, Knudsen-Erath and Tualatin from Oregon.

Wine with Skate
"Thought to be like lobster—by persons of lively imagination" as Meg Dods put it back in 1938. A pleasant if unexciting dish when served with black butter or cheese. Fatty recipes benefit from the appley acidity of sharp, northerly, dry wines.

Wines
Muscadet, Gros Plant, Sancerre, Chablis, Pouilly Fumé, Bourgogne, Aligoté, Coteaux Champenois, Alsace Riesling, German Trockens.

Wine with Brill
Similar to Turbot if not in the same class, this flatfish if cooked in Madeira will take a good fleshy dry wine of some quality.

Recipes
BRILL BAKED WITH CRAYFISH

Wines
Dry Chenin Blanc, including the best Californian, single estate
Graves, the finest Rhône whites, stout Italians like Clastidium,
Fiano di Avellino, Spanish Gran Viña Sol from Penedès, Por-
tuguese Dão and Chardonnays from the best sources.

Wine with Cod

The ubiquitous cod is the mainstay of the British fish industry
and thousands of tons are sold throughout the length and
breadth of the British Isles, usually sprinkled with vinegar and
salt and wrapped in newspaper. Another denizen of northern
seas, cod is an important and inexpensive food and while more
accustomed to strong tea, is not averse to good wine.

Recipes
SWEDISH BOILED COD

Wines
Sylvaner from Alsace, Dry Vouvray, Montlouis, Chablis,
Graves, Gaillac, Bergerac blanc, and the less rarified white
Burgundies, young Graves, Soave, and Orvieto Classico from
Italy and Yugoslavian Zilavka.

Recipes
FISH CURRY, COD WITH SWEET AND SOUR SAUCE

Wines
Very cold, light bodied and fruity whites or reds from the lesser and northerly wine areas of France, Germany and Italy, or indeed anything at all with a spot of character at the cheaper end of the supermarket. Good British cider and beer wouldn't disgrace themselves in this company either.

Recipes
DANISH BAKED COD WITH MUSHROOM SAUCE

Wines
Light fragrant sharp wine, German trockens, crispy Loires, light sharp wines from Saint Bris, Crépy, Pouilly-sur-Loire, Cheverny, Azay-le-Rideau and the Swiss Fendant.

Wine with Hake
If cooked in similar ways to cod use the wines suggested.

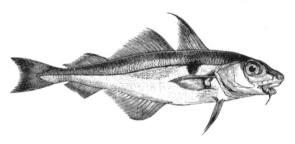

Wine with Haddock
Delicious when prepared at Findon near Aberdeen and sold as Finan Haddock, a golden smokey treat.

Wines
Probably a touch assertive for your best bottles so try instead the soft gentle classics from other countries, the rich creamy Chardonnays, the Italian Donna Marzia and Gavi, the latter made from the unknown (outside Piedmont) Cortese grape, Gran Viña Sol from Penedés, fat Chenins from the likes of Mondavi and Dry Creek in California.

Recipes
**GRILLED FRESH HADDOCK WITH MUSTARD SAUCE,
FILLETS OF HADDOCK WITH LOBSTER CREAM,
FRENCH BAKED HADDOCK AUX "FINES HERBES"**

Wines
Wines of substance, strong whites with character and weight,
Hermitage, Burgundy and Graves, Californian Chardonnays,
Chenins and Sauvignons, Australian Semillon and Chardonnay,
New Zealand Chardonnay, Classico Superiore Soave and the
Hard oxidised wines of Dalmatia.

Recipes
HAM AND HADDIE

Wines
Beaujolais, Chinon, Valpolicella, Bardolino, modest Cabernet or
any mildly interesting and chillable supermarket or corner off-
licence red.

Wine with Whiting
Ideal for those not up to their robust best. A light tasting, slightly
neutral fish which needs sprightly wine to cheer it up.

Recipes
MERLANS BERCY, FRIED WHITING

Wines
Sauvignon Blanc, Gewürztraminer, Grüner-Veltliner, the new
German discoveries Bacchus and Kerner, and old favourite
Müller-Thurgau. Wines made solely from these grapes increasingly state as much on the label. These days it is worthwhile
getting used to the type of wines they make, they are invariably
a cut above the uninspiring blended wines.

Wine with Pouting
If you don't feed it to the cat as *The Sporting Wife* advises, then
use the same recipes and wines as for cod.

Wine with Ling

Recipes
LING, FRIED AND SLICED

Wines
Thick, unctious, full blooded whites, the hefty Chardonnays and other sunny heavyweights.

Wine with Shad
A better class of herring, thus providing good flavoursome food and worthy of nice wine—single estate dry Loires, Graves and dryish German wines of quality.

Recipes
BAKED SHAD

Wines
This recipe is lenient toward fine wine, linger over a good bottle of Burgundy, Grand Cru Graves, first rate Rioja blanca (Murrieta, say), Italian Gavi, Australian, Californian and New Zealand Chardonnay, good German Trockens, fine, good vintage, single estate Chenin or Sauvignon wines from the best Loire producers.

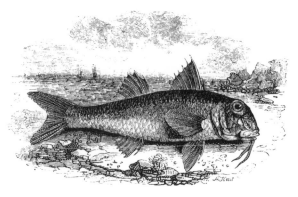

Wine with Mullet

Recipes
RED MULLET

Wines
This delicious inhabitant of the Mediterranean attracts the most diverse wines and has, in its time, been served with Château d'Yquem and Montrachet.

Recipes
ROUGETS À LA NICOISE, ROUGETS AU SAFRAN, BAKED MULLET IN PAPER CASES

Wines
Sicilian wines—Regaleali, Normanno, Corvo Bianco, Etna Bianco, Steri, Rapitalà and Faustus Bianco. Calabrian wines— Cirò Bianco, Squillace, Melissa, and a chilled rosé called Cerasuolo di Vittoria might be just the ticket in that strong sun, if visiting southern Italy.

Wine with Conger Eel
This formidable eel is not as well liked in Britain as it ought to be but providing the ingredients are not too inventive, the conger eel makes a tasty dish which will accommodate wines of flavour and body.

Recipes
STEWED CONGER EEL (IN CIDER)

Wines
Best served with good dry farmhouse cider.

Recipes
SENNEN COVE CONGER STEW (COOKED IN MILK)

Wines
Fragrant sharp wine from the more perfumed grape types— Reisling, Gewürztraminer, Müller-Thurgau, Kerner, Bacchus and Scheurebe.

Recipes
JERSEY CONGER SOUP

Wines
What wine does one serve with marigold flavoured soup? Well,
try medium Montilla, Amontillado Sherry. Sercial Maderia, or
dry white Port.

Wine with Red Gurnard

Recipes
RED GURNARD, BROILED GURNARD, BAKED GURNARD

Wines
This strange sea fish, all spiked armour and able to produce aud-
ible grunts, is less popular these days than of yore. Probably
not worth one's best bottles but it goes well with sharp whites
like Muscadet, Sancerre, Pouilly-Fumé, Aligote and Chablis of
moderate quality and some of the new wave Italian whites like
the Tuscan Galestro.

Wine with Dory

Recipes
JOHN DORY

Wines
Another neglected delicacy in the U.K. but an able companion
to good, fruity wine. Try ripe English, Loire or German.

Recipes
DORY FILLETS FRIED IN BATTER, BOILED DORY

Wines
Good vintage German whites up to Spätlese quality, older bottles will have used up a little of that Süss reserve and should
be better balanced. Try too the medium sweet Chenin Blanc

wines from Touraine, Italian wines labelled amabile or abboccato, Australian Muscats, Californian Ch. La Salle and Tokay
Three Puttonyos.

Wine with Herrings

Recipes
**GRILLED HERRINGS (SERVED WITH MUSTARD SAUCE),
HARENGS AUX BETTERAVES, SOUSED FILLETS OF
HERRING**

Wines
All pretty strongly flavoured recipes. Unless a millionaire, it
would be better to use more modest wines, supermarket whites,
light reds and rosés. Chilled Alsace, Loire, lower Burgundy
(including red and the excellent if lesser known white
Beaujolais), Eastern European whites, Italian wines of the same
quality, the less spectacular Germans, branded American
Chardonnays and Australian Rieslings and Semillons.

Recipes
HERRINGS FRIED IN OATMEAL

Wines
Crisp, acidic Coteaux de Champenois, Alsace varietals, anything
dry from the Loire—Muscadet up river to Sancerre, and all
stations in between. Northern Italian and Swiss whites from
Germanic grape types, Austrian greeny whites and Portuguese
Vinho Verde, even good English wine would not be upstaged
in this company.

Recipes
POTTED HERRINGS

Wines
Any medium dry white with a highish fruit and alcohol content
to counter the vinegar in this dish. Solid, if bland, Bordeaux
or any southern white will suffice.

Wine with Mackerel

This humble fish can be cooked in a number of appetising ways
and is quality food at a very reasonable price. Grilled and served
with butter and parsley it will not detract from good wine.

Recipes
GRILLED MACKEREL

Wines
Chardonnays of great quality, those exquisite buttery, faintly
oaky delights from in particular, the more dependable Burgundy
houses plus a handful of ambitious growers like the Brown
Brothers and Petaluma in Australia, Trefethen, Mondavi and
Chalone in California, Jean Leon in Penedes and Attilio
Simonini in Apulia, Italy. Yes, France had better look to her
laurels in this particular field, the competition is really hotting
up.

Recipes
DRY FRIED MACKEREL

Wines
Plain crisp dry whites—Muscadet sur Lie, lower echelon Chablis, German Kabinetts from the Saar and Mosel, plain value for money Austrian, Bulgarian, Yugoslavian, varietals, popular Italian Verdicchios, Frascatis and Soaves.

Recipes
COLD MACKEREL WITH BRETON SAUCE, SOUSED MACKEREL

Wines
Chilled lager, medium dry cider, or the fruitiest cheap white you can find, Laski Riesling is always cheap and universally available.

Recipes
MACKEREL BALLS

Wines
Fragrant whites from the more scented grapes—Riesling, Müller-Thurgau, and Gewürztraminer from Alsace, Austria, Germany, Northern Italy, England and Fruska Gora (Yugoslavia).

Wine with Dog Fish

Recipes
CURRIED DOG FISH, GARLIC DOG FISH

Wines
Delicious fruity rosé d'Anjou de Cabernet

Wine with Bass

Recipes
POACHED BASS

Wines
This fine fish comes in various guises, Black, White, Calico, Sea, Stone, even Striped and is worth an exceptional wine. Fine Chardonnay, Sauvignon Blanc wines from the best, sufficiently eulogised exponents of these fine grapes in the world. The Ligurians, on the other hand, prefer to drink Vermentino with their Branzino in tegame (a local dish of Mediterranean Sea Bass cooked in white wine, tomato and herbs).

Wine with Sprats
Smoked, or grilled Sprats are a delicious prelude to a fine meal and they deserve a light neutral wine, fresh with some acidity, but low in alcohol. Hypermarket boxed plonk or similar should be shunned in favour of a crisp Muscadet, young Chablis or delicious Sancerre.

Recipes
SAVOURY SPRATS, SPRATS FRIED IN BATTER, BAKED SPRATS AND ANCHOVY

Wines
Muscadet, Gros Plant, Aligoté, sharp, young, off vintage Chablis, bone dry German Trockens, the delightful mountainous wines of Valle d'Aosta or the scented, thirst quenching attractions of the Trentino–Alto Adige area in Northern Italy.

Wine with Pilchard
Out of tins and normally soused in tomato sauce, an ordinary wine will suffice to see them off. Any light red Chinon, Beaujolais, Valpolicella, Bardolino, young modern Rioja, crisp Cabernets from outside the great areas, there are endless possibilities, but do find something with a suggestion of quality, look for VDQS, A/C, or DOC on the label.

Wine with Whitebait

Recipes
FRIED WHITEBAIT

Wines
Delightfully fragrant white from the best and most stylish grape types, Riesling, Sauvignon (good Sancerre is the best example in the world). Kabinett Mosels and Austrian Grüner-Veltliner.

Wine with Lobster
This splendid crustacean prefers, according to one of those earnest American experiments, being put into cold water and heated to death rather than a sudden and violent immersion in boiling water. However, lobster is delicious and quite suitable company for the best and creamiest whites.

Recipes
LOBSTER THERMIDOR

Wines
Gourmands have, on occasion, served everything from the very finest Sauternes to the best dry Graves with this dish and only experimentation will settle the argument as to which is the better choice. A decent, dry wine with a goodly proportion of fruit acid would be preferable as a counter balance to all that tomato purée, butter and grated cheese. Sancerre (the finest estate bottled wines), Coteaux de Champenois, Alsace Riesling, Gewürztraminer, and Muscat of the best vintages, Premier Cru Chablis and the wonderful Spätlesen wines of the Rheingau (from such masters as Schönborn von Brentano and Graf Matuschka-Greiffenclau).

Recipes
BOILED LOBSTER

Wines
The best and most flavoursome Chardonnays from the finest
growers in the world, by now you should know some key names.

Recipes
**SOUFFLÉ OF LOBSTER À LA DIABLE, MEXICAN
LOBSTER**

Wines
Eggs, vinegar, mustard, anchovy essence, cream and tabasco.
Not ingredients to set before a fine expensive wine unless it is
absolutely massive, and one is rich enough to drink great wines
every day (and how utterly boring that would be!). Large
Rhônes, Premier and Grand Cru Chablis of the best years, Gran
Viña Sol and Chardonnay from Penedès, Portuguese Dão
branco, Gavi dei Gavi and Terre Rosse Chardonnay from Italy,
and the lumbering Chardonnays from California.

Wine with Crab
This may seem a strange and unattractive creature to look at
in a seaside rock pool but crab meat is delicious to eat. The
flesh is usually mixed with oil and seasonings to give its mild
taste an edge. The simplest recipe involves little adjustment to
the natural flavour and is the best way to serve it with fine wine.

Wines
Delicate, mature Burgundies or Graves, or a decent Spätlesen,
Mosel or Saar wine with a few years in bottle would suit
admirably.

Recipes
BOILED CRAB, DRESSED

Wines
Fine delicate wines with a crisp, fresh finish, young Mosel,
Alsace Muscat, and Riesling, the best of the Loire Sauvignons,

Austrian Grüner-Veltliner, and Oregon wines of Germanic origins. Spider crab is popular in Italy and they eat it with the dry, fruity wines of the area. In Veneto, for example, with a dish called "Granseola alla veneziana" (spider crab prepared with oil and lemon) they go for the locally grown Bianco di Custoza, a light dry white wine made from a mixture of several of Italy's best known grapes. In Fruili-Venezia Giulia, on the other hand, they like their "Granzevola alla triestina" (spider crab cooked in breadcrumbs, garlic and herbs) with their highly respected Tocai and Pinot Bianco. Incidentally, wines made from a number of different grapes tend not to have the quality on the nose of the classic single grape wines, great claret is the unique exception.

Recipes
CRABMEAT CASSEROLE, CRAB NEWBURG

Wines
Good, hard, flinty whites with a balanced acidity—big Rieslings from Alsace, the best Sancerres, Madame Joly's wonderful late picked, but bone dry, Chenin Blanc, or greeny-gold Chablis up to Premier Cru standard.

Wine with Crayfish
Freshwater crayfish grilled over coals is called "Gamberi d'acqua ai ferri" in the Italian region of Molise. With it they drink a modest white wine called Vernaccia di Serra Meccaglia. Not tied to the wines of just one area or country we may do as we please and select instead any number of the lovely wines from the packed shelves of our High Street shops, everything from the finest Chardonnays of Burgundy to the minor delights of Bulgaria. The Sauvignon, alas, is not the great traveller that Chardonnay is so the best bottles tend to be made on its home soil in France. Northern Sauvignons will have that extra crispness favoured on a beautiful sunny day in mid summer, while the more substantial wines of Bordeaux and California will do nicely in the depths of winter.

Wine with Oyster

This mysterious creature comes in a profusion of nationalities but the Colchester native is certainly one of the best. I prefer to eat oysters without the addition of Tabasco and Worcestershire sauces, cayenne pepper, garlic or even lemon juice. Wine of reasonable quality if desirable with plain snapped-open-and-slid-down-the-gullet oysters. If the cook starts doing things to ginger up the recipes then we must turn to the appropriate wines. Try Tokay d'Alsace, Coteaux Champenois Blanc or the interestingly dry Doisy-Daëne, from a famous Barsac producer.

Recipes
ANGELS ON HORSEBACK, FRIED OYSTERS

Wines
Light, sharp, green wines from the shadier areas on the wine map. Anything from the upper halves of France, Italy and Portugal, German Kabinett from the Mosel and Nahe, and the light modern wines of South Africa, Oregon and Australia.

Recipes
OYSTER STEW

Wines
Good reds from sunnier vineyards, anything from Bordeaux, the Rhône, Piedmont, Tuscany, Spain, Portugal and our friends in the New World.

Wine with shrimps and Prawns

Recipes
SHRIMP DE JONGHE, CREAMED SHRIMPS, SHRIMP RAREBIT

Wines
Grüner-Veltliner, Hungarian Badacsony, Yugoslavian Zilavka, Riesling and Traminer, Italian Tocai and Pinot Bianco from Friuli-Venezia Giulia, the dry and perfumed Esmeralda from Penedès and good dry Vinho Verde.

Recipes
**PRAWNS IN SOYA SAUCE, PEAR AND PRAWN CURRY,
SPICED FRIED PRAWNS OR SHRIMPS, CURRIED
PRAWNS**

Wines
Rich and humble wine from southern France, Spain, Italy, Portugal and Greece, indeed neutral quaffing wine, red, white or
pink, from anywhere.

Recipes
FRIED SCAMPI

Wines
Delicious gooseberry flavoured Sancerre, or Pouilly Fumé, as
I have already said an estate bottled version is worth that little
extra, the wines of Jean Vatan (Sancerre) and Jean-Claude
Guyot (Pouilly Blanc Fumé) are recommended.

Recipes
PRAWN PATTIES

Wines
Fresh cool grapey wines from the mittel Mosel, Saar, the lesser
Rheingaus, plus imitations of the same from California, Austra-
lia and Italy.

Wine with Scallops
This mollusc will go nicely with wines of character and quality,
but the better and more elegant bottles should be reserved for
the Baked recipe.

Recipes
COQUILLES SAINT JACQUES À LA BRETONNE

Wines
This recipe includes butter, brandy and white wine, so something crisp with a bit of body is what's required—Chablis, Rully, good Macon blanc from the better villages (Lugny, Viré, Azé, Clessé, Igé and Verzé), also the recently emerged Saint Véran which is a blend of the better Chardonnay wines from around Pouilly-Fuissé and Beaujolais Blanc, Alsace varietals, Vouvray, Sancerre, Pouilly Fumé, Austrian dry whites, German Kabinetts and the fresh Italian wines of Valle d'Aosta, Trentino-Alto Adige and Friuli-Venezia Giulia.

Recipes
BAKED SCALLOPS

Wines
A simple preparation this but go gently with that traditional enemy of fine wine, lemon juice. The best Rieslings, Chardonnays, Chenins and Sauvignons, plus the neglected white wine of the Rhône Valley—the beautiful but expensive Viognier wines of the north and the wines of Hermitage and Châteauneuf du Pape squeezed from the unglamorous Marsanne and Rousanne grapes, also the best German, Italian, Spanish, Portuguese, Austrian, American, Australian and New Zealand dry white wines.

Wine with Mussels

Recipes
MOULES À LA MARINIÈRE, MUSSEL PILAF, MUSSEL PUDDING

Wines
Deliciously evocative, reminding one of perfumed breezes and sunny days by the sea, fresh light summery wines of every hue will do. British wine shippers import many cheap country varietals these days which are also extremely cheerful.

Wine with Lamprey
Why anyone would want to eat something that might poison them is beyond my comprehension, however, if you are tempted then make what may turn out to be your last bottle this side of Heaven a very good one!

Recipes
LAMPREYS MATELOTE

Wines
Use the same red wine the fish is cooked in, if a good one, otherwise select a decent claret or claret type from one of the better Cabernet Sauvignon growers, i.e. Marchesi Incisa della Rochetta (Tuscany) and Giorgio Gray (Trentino) of Italy, Robert Mondavi, Joe Heitz from the Napa Valley, Château Tahbilk in Australia, Cooks in New Zealand, or Château Musar from the troubled Lebanon.

Recipes
STUFFED LAMPREY

Wines
Pinot Noir Rosé from Marsannay or Alsace, the light pinky reds of Germany, the Austrian Saint Laurent, and the sharp fruity reds of the Loire.

Wine with Cockles
The self same thing that Molly Malone sold off her barrow in "the streets broad and narrow" of my native Dublin. An able substitute for mussels in fish sauces and delightful in soup with celery, milk and butter.

Recipes
COCKLE SOUP

Wines
Medium or dry Montilla or Sherry, Sercial, dry Vin Santo, Tokay from Szamorodni up to Three Puttonyos, dry white Port, Château-Chalon and Vin Jaune.

Wine with Fish and Chips
It is hard to argue with *The Sporting Wife's* suggestion that a cup of strong tea is the proper partner to dear old English Fish and Chips. The delicious flavour of fish and chips comes from the lard traditionally used to fry them, although *Daily Mirror* headlines may also have something to do with it! Whatever the reason, to middle-aged romantics a newspaper full of steaming fish and chips shared with a loved one in a battered Mini was one of the great culinary delights of one's youth. The more prosaic of course may use plates and cutlery and even a bottle of dry, fairly tart white wine, but it will not be the same.

Recipes
FISH PIE

Wines
Pluck a modest red or white wine from your nearest supermarket for this humble fare.

Wine with Roe

Recipes
HERRING ROE, SAVOURY FRITTERS OF HERRING ROES, HERRING ROES À LA MODE, HERRING ROE PUFFS, DEVILLED SOFT HERRING ROES, BOILED COD'S ROE, FRIED SHAD ROE, DRIED MULLET ROE, ROE AS A SUBSTITUTE FOR CAVIAR

Wines
Brisk whites or rosés from the fruitier grapes—Riesling, Muscat, Sauvignon, Müller-Thurgau, and northerly Chardonnays, and for the pink wines Pinot Noir, Cabernet Franc, Lagrein, Nerello Mascalese, Lambrusco and Gamay.

Recipes
FRESHWATER BOUILLABAISSE

Wines
Good quality fresh tasting whites (the Italians like their Treb-

bianos, Verdicchios and Vermentinos), but Muscadet,
Sauvignon, Sylvaner, Chardonnay and young white Rioja wines
are equally adaptable.

Recipes
RISOTTO AUX FRUITS DE MER

Wines
Essentially an Italian creation so why not stick to the excellent
wines of its native country—Soave, Frascati, Verdicchio,
Vermentino, Locorotondo (one of the better Appulian wines),
Tocai, Verduzzo secco, Ramitello and Ischia Bianco, and
Regaleali and Rapitalà, a couple of biancos from Sicily.

Recipes
BISQUE

Wines
Vouvray, white Rhônes, Graves, Soave Classico, southern
Chardonnays.

Recipes
FISH CHOWDER, FISH CAKES

Wines
Chardonnays from the sunny south, Californian Chenin Blancs, Steen (same thing) from South Africa, Semillons from Australia, German Sylvaners.

Recipes
KEDGEREE, CLASSIC KEDGEREE

Wines
Originally an Indian dish and if served as a midday meal then good quality rosé, cool fragrant grapey white, or even a chilled light red would be appropriate.

Recipes
GEFILTE FISH, FISH TIMBALE

Wines
Rich dryish whites from Burgundy, the Palatinate and Baden, white oaky Riojas, Gran Viña Sol and Chardonnay from Penedès, silky Italian white Masianco, Vernaccia di San Gimignano, Etna Bianco superiore, Dão branco from Portugal, Californian Fumé Blanc, Chenin Blanc and Chardonnay, Australian Château Tahbilk (Marsanne), Robson Vineyard's Chardonnay.

Recipes
SMOKED FISH PÂTÉ

Wines
Why not encourage local industry and opt for a home produced wine? In spite of our unsympathetic climate some quite decent wine is made in England but not every year in spite of recent successes in wine tasting competitions versus the French third or fourth eleven. Our grape types are generally of a Teutonic type and the wines reflect this bias. Those bearing the gold seal

of the English Vineyards' Association tend to be better having passed both analytical and organoleptic tests before going on sale, and now that some of the early novelty has worn off English wine prices are keener and distribution is better. Most English wine growers are based in the slightly sunnier southern counties but quite good wine is being produced as far north as Hereford-shire and Gloucestershire.

TYPE, PRICE RANGE AND AVAILABILITY OF SOME SUGGESTED WINES

Key
R = Red   W = White   Rs = Rosé   Spk = Sparkling   Amb = Amber   Yel = Yellow   Oxid = Oxidised

Countries of Origin
Aust = Australia   Aus = Austria   Arg = Argentina   Bulg = Bulgaria   Calif = California   Chil = Chile   Eng = England   Fr = France   Ger = Germany   Gr = Greece   Hung = Hungary   It = Italy   Leb = Lebanon   N.Z. = New Zealand   Ore = Oregon   Port = Portugal   Rom = Romania   Sp = Spain   Swi = Switzerland   S.A. = South Africa,   Yug = Yugoslavia

Approximate Prices
A—Inexpensive wines for everyday drinking   B—Moderately priced wines of good quality   C—Fine wines, good value   D—Rare, superb and inevitably pricey.

Where to buy
Trad = Traditional Wine Merchants, i.e. reputable, honest and well established wine companies carrying a wide range of interesting wines, producing informative and up to date lists, and usually offering courteous service and deliveries. Spec = Usually small well run family firms specialising in the wine of one particular country, as a result of which they become experts in a narrow field and carry unusual and interesting items often produced in too small a quantity to interest larger firms.

W/A = Widely Available indicates the wine concerned is likely to appear on supermarket shelves, in off-licence windows, and maybe even in among the soap powders, cat food and wax candles of the licensed corner shop. For everyday items, and increasingly for the better wine too, the supermarket has come of age and is normally efficiently run if, at times, lacking the point of sale information and pleasant knowing confidence of the traditional wine man.

If time permits, a little shopping around is advised as prices, shippers, vintages and indeed quality varies from one outlet to the next. Wine is a huge, fascinating and ever-changing subject and good bottles may be found in the most unlikely places. A morning spent for example at a wine auction can be an amusing and worthwhile experience and good bottles may be purchased quite cheaply in one's and two's or mixed cases.

Even in these enlightened times out of condition bottles regularly turn up. Do not hesitate to return poor wines. Supermarket wines have a short life so there is little point buying these for storing at home. Drink them as soon as possible. As for older more venerable items, they also, alas, decline so try not to hoard old wines too long imagining they are worth a fortune, single bottles seldom are unless of course they are very rare and in mint condition. Tasting wines in advance of purchase is desirable but not often possible, however, wine societies, groups and certain merchants occasionally organise tastings for their customers. A list of these and other useful diary dates are frequently to be seen in the specialist wine magazines.

Wine	Colour	Country	Comments	Price	Avail
AGLIANICO DEL VULTURE	R	*It. Basilicata*	Potentially excellent, mahogany coloured red from southern Italy.	B	Spec
ALIGOTÉ	W	*Fr. Burgundy*	Ordinary grape making light acidic whites.	B	W/A
AMONTILLADO	Amb	*Sp. Jerez*	At best full-flavoured, nutty and satisfying	A. B	W/A
ANJOU ROSÉ DE CABERNET	Rs	*Fr. Loire*	Semi sweet rosé, a cut above plain Anjou pink.	B	Trad
ARBIN	R	*Fr. Savoie*	Dark irony wine for drinking young.	A	Trad
ASTI SPUMANTE	Spk	*It. Piedmont*	Fruity, fizzy and much loved muscatel flavoured sparkler.	B	W/A
AZAY-LE-RIDEAU	W	*Fr. Loire*	Razor sharp Chenin Blanc from a popular Loire village	A	Trad
BACCHUS	W	*Ger.*	Registered since 1961 this Sylvaner/Riesling/Müller-Thurgau cross is highly spiced (hardly surprising with that parentage).	B. C	Trad
BADACSONY	W	*Hung. Balaton*	High grown, full bodied, medium dry wine of consistent quality.	A	Trad
BAIRRADA	R	*Port. Beira Littoral*	Everyday reds and whites and modest bubbly.	A. B	Trad
BARBARESCO	R	*It. Piedmont*	At times the best of all the fine Nebbiolo wines, very reasonably priced too.	C. D	W/A
BARBERA	R	*It. Piedmont*	Normally an ordinary red wine but the one from Lombardy has potential.	A. B	W/A
BARCA VELHA	R	*Port. Tras-Os-Montes*	A rich mature red that holds out some hope for the unheralded Portuguese table wines.	B	Spec

Wine	Colour	Country	Comments	Price	Avail
BARDOLINO	R	*It.* *Veneto*	Popular light red, the Classico Superiore is best.	A. B	W/A
BAROLO	R	*It.* *Piedmont*	Huge and unyielding at times but great vintages can with sympathetic cellaring become fabulously smooth.	C	W/A
BEAUJOLAIS	R. W	*Fr.* *Burgundy*	Deliciously fragrant lightweight, often drunk either too young or too old. The Crus (Fleurie, Moulin-à-Vent etc.) are excellent value.	A/C	W/A
BEAUNE	R. W Spk	*Fr.* *Burgundy*	Fine Pinot Noirs and Chardonnays in good years, the Premier Crus are worth investigating.	B–D	W/A
BELI PINOT	W	*Yug.*	Unpretentious drink, smooth, cheap and uncomplicated.	A	Trad
BERGERAC	R. W	*Fr.* *Dordogne*	Similar to minor wines of Bordeaux.	A. B	W/A
BERNKASTEL	W	*Ger.* *Mosel*	Popular often insipid and sweetish whites, the single estate unsugared wines however are excellent.	A–D	W/A
BIANCO DI CUSTOZA	W	*It.* *Veneto*	Useful smooth dry white.	A. B	Trad
BLANC DE COSSON	W	*It.* *Valle d'Aosta*	Crisp white for immediate despatch.	B	Spec
BLANC DE MORGEX	W	*It.* *Valle d'Aosta*	Sharp, low strength white, good aperitif or picnic wine.	B	Spec
BLANC DE SALLE	W	*It.* *Valle D'Aosta*	Cool mountainy fish wine.	B	Spec
BLAUFRÄN-KISCH	R	*Aus.*	Pleasant light red from the Gamay grape.	A	Trad

Wine	Colour	Country	Comments	Price	Avail
BLAYE	R	*Fr. Bordeaux*	Similar to Bourg, Modest but reliable mini clarets.	A. B	W/A
BOCA	R	*It. Piedmont*	Another if lesser Nebbiolo wine from Piedmont.	B. C.	W/A
BOGDANUSA	W	*Yug.*	One to bring back from holiday, cheap and appetising dry white.	A	Spec
BONARDA	R	*It. Lombardy and elsewhere*	Tough, swarthy red.	A. B	Spec
BORDEAUX	R. W. Rs. Spk	*Fr.*	An area boasting the highest proportion of fine wines in the world, notably the great clarets and sauternes.	A–D	W/A
BOURG	R	*Fr. Bordeaux*	Minor clarets, the Côtes or hill bred versions are a fraction more complex.	A. B	W/A
BRAMATERRA	R	*It. Piedmont*	Good reds from the Nebbiolo grape but with limited keeping potential.	A. B	Spec
BRICCO MANZONI	R	*It. Piedmont*	Nice rare red from the classic Nebbiolo and the artisan Barbera grapes.	B. C	Spec
BRUNELLO DI MONTALCINO	R	*It. Tuscany*	Fine firm red, for discerning palates.	C–D	Trad
BUCELAS	W	*Port. Estra-madura*	Pleasant if modest dry whites.	A. B	Trad
BULL'S BLOOD	R	*Hung. Eger*	Mass produced once earthy red now tamed for a wider market.	A	W/A
BURGUNDY	R. W. Rs. Spk	*Fr.*	Fine area noted for expensive and inconsistent reds and some heavenly Chardonnays.	B–D	W/A

Wine	Colour	Country	Comments	Price	Avail
CABERNET FRANC	R	*Fr. Bulg, It. Hung. Yug.*	Light, crisp, perfumed red.	A	W/A
CABERNET SAUVIGNON		*Bulg. Hung. Arg. Chil. It. Cali. Sp. Ore. Aust. N.Z. Aus.*	Portugal and Germany have yet to join the club but the greatest grape on earth makes wine which at worst is pleasant and interesting, at best the epitome of greatness.	A–D	W/A
CAHORS	R	*Fr. S. West*	This once rich black wine is now merely an ordinary red for everyday drinking.	A. B	W/A
CALDARO	R	*It. Trentino*	Classic Caldaro is grapey and uncomplicated wine for al fresco fare.	A	Trad
CALIFORNIAN	R. W. Rs. Spk	*U.S.*	Smooth strong wines often lacking the sharp definition of the great European names they unashamedly ape. Napa Valley is their Médoc, Nuits St. Georges, Alsace and Rhine, and their best wines come close at times especially when young.	A–D	Spec/ Trad
CAMPO FIORIN	R	*It. Veneto*	A superior Valpolicella with body and strength.	C	Spec
CAÑAMERO	W	*Sp. Estram- adura*	Spain's answer to Château-Chalon, strong, oxidised aperitifs.	C	Spec
CANNONAU	R. W	*Sardinia*	Variable, quite interesting at times.	A	Spec
CAPITAL SAN ROCCO	R. W	*It. Veneto*	Good strong red and sharpish white.	B. C	Spec
CARAMINO	R	*It. Piedmont*	Another fine Nebbiolo wine from the Piedmont treasure trove of fine Italian reds.	B	Spec

Wine	Colour	Country	Comments	Price	Avail
CAREMA	R	*It. Piedmont*	Lovely Nebbiolo wine, a hilly cousin of Barolo.	B	Trad
CARMIGNANO	R	*It. Tuscany*	Another variation on the Chianti theme here with a little Cabernet the wine is long lasting and potentially quite fine.	B. C	Spec
CASTEL DANIELIS	R	*Gr.*	Humble rough red.	A	Trad
CASTELLO DI RONCADE	R	*It. Veneto*	A praiseworthy attempt to make claret using Bordeaux grape types.	B	Spec
CERASUOLO DI SCILLA	Rs	*It. Calabria*	Interesting pinky reds.	B	Spec
CHABLIS	W	*Fr.*	Sharp, flavoursome Chardonnay, the best (Grand Cru) can be brilliant middleweights.	C. D	Trad
CHAMPAGNE	Spk. R. W. Rs.	*Fr. Champagne*	The first and best bubbly in the world ranging from the austere to the ethereal. Krug is the benchmark, luxurious and expensive.	D	Trad
CHANTURGES	R	*Fr. Central*	Light picnic red from the Beaujolais vine	A	Trad
CHARDONNAY	W	*Burg. Bulg. Sp. It. Aust. U.S.A. and elsewhere*	The finest and creamiest dry wine grape of all, a versatile traveller coming up to scratch almost everywhere.	B–D	W/A
CHÂTEAU-CHALON	Yel. Oxid.	*Fr. Jura*	Expensive, dried out wine with a salty tang and a taste that has to be acquired.	D	Trad
CHÂTEAUNEUF-DU-PAPE	R. W	*Fr. Rhône*	Fine, rich, distinguished reds when from traditional, family run estates (Brunier, Perrin, and Baron Le Roy de Boiseaumarié are just three great names).	C. D	W/A

Wine	Colour	Country	Comments	Price	Avail
CHENIN BLANC	W	*Fr. S.A. Cali. N.Z.*	A versatile and potentially long lived grape, honeyed when overripe yet capable of wine that swerves from luscious to bone dry. Excels only along the Loire where a ripe and fruity acidity gives it bite and flavour.		
CHIANTI	R	*It. Tuscany*	Famous reds representing the peaks and troughs of Italian wine making.	A–D	W/A
CHEVERNY	W	*Fr. Loire*	Acidic refreshers.	A	Trad
CHINON	R	*Fr. Loire*	Romantic picnic reds, endearing aromatic lightweights.	B. C	W/A
CHUSCLAN	R. W.	*Fr. Rhône*	Reliable if one dimensional.	A	W/A
CINQUETERRE	W	*It. Liguria*	Ancient name but not turning on the poets anymore	A	Trad
CIRO	W	*It. Calabrian*	Dry with moderate fruit.	B. C	Spec
CLARET	R	*Fr. Bordeaux*	The general term for the red wines of Bordeaux, covers a vast range of wines from the everyday to the magnificent.	A–D	W/A
CLASTIDIUM	W	*It. Lombardy*	Unusual and almost unobtainable oaky white.	C	Spec
COLARES	R	*Port.*	Over-rated stringy red.	A	Spec
CONDRIEU	W	*Fr. Rhône*	Flowery, pricey and occasionally unreliable dry whites.	D	Trad
COOKS CABERNET	R	*N.Z.*	North Island elegant red approaching in quality the lower reaches of classified clarets.	B	W/A

Wine	Colour	Country	Comments	Price	Avail
CORNAS	R	*Fr.* *Rhône*	Excellent and little known full bodied red.	B. C	Trad
COTNARI	W. Oxid	*Rom.* *Moldavia*	Legendary, oxidised and sweet.	B	Trad
CORTON	R. W.	*Fr.* *Burgundy*	Wonderful and costly wines of both colours when on top form.	D	Trad
CÔTES DE BUZET	R. W	*Fr.* *S. West*	Bordeaux style lightweights, reliable enough but seldom exciting.	A. B	W/A
CÔTE CHALONNAISE	R. W	*Fr.* *Burgundy*	Lesser Burgundies of both hues, never exceptional but there are bargains among the bland.	B. D	W/A
CÔTES DE DURAS	R. W	*Fr.* *Dordogne*	Modest Cabernet inspired reds and bland whites.	A. B	W/A
COTEAUX DU LAYON	W	*Fr.* *Loire*	Sharply sweet long lasting whites.	A–D	Trad
CÔTE DE NUITS	R	*Fr.* *Burgundy*	A wide range of Pinot Noirs from thin ordinaires to rich extraordinaires. The best are wonderfully opulent, elegant and memorable.	A–D	W/A
CÔTE RÔTIE	R	*Fr.* *Rhône*	France's smoothest richest red, delicious when young, divine when mature.	C–D	W/A
CORVO BIANCO	W	*It.* *Sicily*	Dry, good considering the climate.	B. C	Spec
COTEAUX CHAMPENOISE	R. W	*Fr.* *Champagne*	Delightfully refreshing hilly still wines, tart, sharp, and they keep surprisingly well.	B. C	Trad
COTEAUX DU TRICASTIN	R. W	*Fr.* *Rhône*	More medium quality, reliable and inexpensive wine.	A	W/A

Wine	Colour	Country	Comments	Price	Avail
CRÉPY	W	*Fr. Savoie*	Light and trendy holiday wine.	B	Trad
CUBZAC	R. W	*Fr. Bordeaux*	Yet more mini clarets, at best pleasantly elegant.	A. B	W/A
DOLCETTO	R	*It. Piedmont*	From light and crisp to heavy reds.	A. B	Spec
DÔLE	R	*Swi.*	Expensive for what they are but pleasantly fruity.	A	Spec
DÃO	R. W	*Port. Viseu*	Solid, plain reds older bottles improve	A. B	W/A
DINGAC	R	*Yug. Dalmatia*	Massive "Porty" red, good with assertive native food.	A	Spec
DOMAINE CHANDON	W	*Calif. Napa Valley*	Good but pricey salute to Champagne.	D	Spec
DOMAINES DES IDEAUDIÈRE	W. Spk	*Fr. Loire*	Sharp, sparkling, and soft Vouvrays.	B. C	W/A
DONNA MARZIA	W. R	*It. Apulia*	Surprising quality reds and whites from Italy's high heel.	B	Spec
CH. DOISY-DAËNE	W	*Fr. Sauternes*	Crisp and fruity when dry.	B	Trad
DRY CREEK	R. W	*Calif. Sonoma*	Rich Chardonnays and Chenins.	C. D	Spec
EASTERN BLOC	R. W Rs. Spk		Cheap source of improving wines of quality and variety.	A	W/A
EDELZWICKER	W	*Fr. Alsace*	Standard mixture, strong, dry and sound.	A. B	W/A
ENGLISH	W		At best fresh and fragrant, medium sweet to sharply dry.	A. B	W/A
ENTRE-DEUX-MERS	W	*Fr. Bordeaux*	Crisper than of yore.	A	W/A
ESMERALDA	W	*Sp. Penedès*	Skilful and appetizing blend of Muscat and Gewürztraminer.	A	W/A

Wine	Colour	Country	Comments	Price	Avail
ETNA BIANCO SUPERIORE	R. W Rs.	*Sicily*	Strapping golden and dry.	A. B	Spec
EZERJÓ	W	*Hung.*	Pleasant, dryish and spicey.	A	Trad
FALERNO	R. W	*It. Latium*	Robust red with potential, white is dry and nondescript.	A	Spec
FARA	R	*It. Piedmont*	Elegant red, when cellared.	A. B	Spec
FARO	R	*Yug. Dalmatia*	Massive wine, a match for spicey stews and other strong fare. N.B. Also known as Sicilian red.	A	Spec
FAUSTUS	R. W Rs.	*It. Sicily*	Brand name for a useful and interesting range of reds, whites, and rosés.	A	Spec
FAVONIO	R. W	*It. Apulia*	Surprising quality from the deep south.	A. B	Spec
FENDANT	W	*Swi.*	An ordinary Swiss white from a limited grape called Chasselas in France.	A	Spec
FIANO DI AVELLINO	W	*It. Campania*	Good nutty white.	B	Spec
FINE WINE	R. W	*Fr. Ger. It.*	Wine of exceptional flavour, balance and pure drinkability, can be sweet, dry, red, white, fortified (i.e. Port) or Champagne. Calif. Sp. Leb. Aust. and N.Z. are on the horizon and catching up.	C+	W/A
FINO	Oxid	*Sp.*	Elegant, smooth, bone to off dry sherry.	A. B	W/A
FIORANO	R	*It. Latium*	Elegant red with Bordeaux leanings.	B	Spec
FRASCATI	W	*It. Latium*	Yellow, smooth and famous with a slightly sunburnt flavour.	A	W/A
FREEMARK ABBEY	R. W	*Calif. Napa*	Carefully made French style wines.	C	W/A

Wine	Colour	Country	Comments	Price	Avail
LA ROCHE AUX MOINES	W	*Fr.* *Loire*	Fabulous nobly ripened, and fulsome dry white.	C. D	Trad
LAVILLE-HAUT-BRION	W	*Fr.* *Bordeaux*	Yellow, satiny, fine Graves.	D	Trad
LEANYKA	W	*Hung.*	Balanced little white, eminently drinkable.	A	W/A
LIMBERGER	R	*Ger.*	Sharp, refreshing reds.	A	Spec
LIRAC	R. W. Rs.	*Fr.* *Rhône*	Solid dry pinks and reds.	A	W/A
LOCOROTONDO	W	*It.* *Apulia*	Crisp tasty white from Southern Italy.	A. B	Spec
LOUPIAC	W	*Fr.* *Bordeaux*	Light, shadowy Sauternes type, sweet wines.	A. B	W/A
LUGANA	W. Spk	*It.* *Lombardy*	The still version is dry, balanced, fresh and flavoursome.	B	Spec
MACON	R. W	*Fr.* *Burgundy*	Drinkable reds and whites of ordinary quality.	A	W/A
MALAGA	Amb	*Sp.* *Malaga*	A plebeian pudding wine, the older versions are better.	A	W/A
MALBEC	R	*Yug. Fr.* *Calif. It.*	Soft, gentle reds for quick drinking, also contributes to great claret.	A. B	Trad
MALVASIA	W	*Fr. and elsewhere*	Sweetish and mild or caramelly and rich depending on location.		W/A
MALVASIA DELLA LIPARI	Amb	*It.* *Sicily*	Pudding wines ranging from sweet to treacly, but reliable.	B	Spec
MANZANILLA	Yel	*Sp.* *Jerez*	The best aperitif in the world, dry, pure and satisfying.	A. B	W/A
MAREGIA	W	*It.* *Emilia Romagna*	Dry light white of some quality.	A	Spec

Wine	Colour	Country	Comments	Price	Avail
MARFIL	W. R	*Sp. Catalonia*	Modest red and white branded wines.	A	W/A
MARINO	W	*It. Latium*	Frascati's first cousin, the dry wood-aged and fairly strong version is Superiore.	A. B	Spec
CÔTES DU MARMANDAIS	R	*Fr. Dordogne*	Shadowy clarets and undistinguished whites.	A	Trad
MARSALA	Amb	*It. Sicily*	All things to all men, but the older, drier versions are quite interesting.	A. B	W/A
MARSANNAY	R. Rs	*Fr. Burgundy*	This dry oniony-skin coloured rosé is a quite serious wine for buffs.	A	Trad
MARSANNE	W	*Fr. Rhône*	Makes strong gold-tinted dry wine.	B. C	W/A
ROUSANNE	W	*Fr. Rhône*	Usually twinned with Marsanne to make strong one dimensional wines but there are sumptious wood-aged exceptions.	B. C	W/A
MAVRO REMEIKO	R	*Gr. Crete*	Dark, strong, unpretentious stuff.	A	Trad
MAVRUD	R	*Bulg.*	Strongly flavoured dark red, with some depth.	A	Trad
MELISSA	R. W	*It. Calabria*	This sweet sounding wine is fairly big when red, and soft and gentle when white.	B	Spec
MERLOT	R	*Fr. Bordeaux and elsewhere*	Makes soft, very acceptable, unassuming wine on its own, but with a little Cabernet, i.e. St. Emilion and Pomerol can be very fine indeed.	C	Spec
MEURSAULT	W	*Fr. Burgundy*	Fine and creamy when of a good vintage, so-so otherwise.	C. D	Trad

Wine	Colour	Country	Comments	Price	Avail
MIDI	R. W Rs	*Fr.*	Warm and ordinary but the EEC is forcing improvements.	A	W/A
MONBAZILLAC	W	*Fr.* *Dordogne*	Light Sauternes style wine.	A	W/A
MONTECARLO	W	*It.* *Tuscany*	A fair blend of native and French grapes.	B	Spec
MONTEL-PULCIANO DEL MOLISE	R	*It.* *Molise*	Interesting red from this lesser known Italian region.	A	Spec
MONTILLA	Yel. Amb	*Sp.* *Montilla*	Used to be called sherry, now fends for itself quite successfully, extremely good value.	A	W/A
MONTLOUIS	W	*Fr.* *Loire*	Less famous than Vouvray but better than some.	A	W/A
MONTRACHET [LE]	W	*Fr.* *Burgundy*	When it attains the superb heights of a 1978 or a 1982 then it is very expensive and very good, probably the best dry white of all.	D	Trad
MORIO MUSCAT	W	*Ger.*	Usually sweet, perfumed and pretty forgetable.	A. B	Trad
MOULIN-TOUCHAIS	W	*Fr.* *Loire*	Family firm specialising in sharply sweet wines at bargain prices.	B	W/A
MÜLLERREBE	R	*Ger.*	A light delicate red.	A	Trad
MÜLLER-THURGAU	W	*Ger.*	Perfumed lightweights, the popular U.K. taste in German wine.	A	W/A
MUSAR [CH]	R	*Leb.*	Excellent stylish red from a surprising source.	C. D	W/A
MUSCADET	W	*Fr.* *Loire*	Sharp dry and acidic, seldom better.	A	W/A
MUSCAT D'ALSACE	W	*Fr.* *Alsace*	Beautiful, perfumed bone dry wine from one of the sweetest grapes of all.	A. B	W/A
MUSKAT-OTTONEL	W	*Aus*	Sweet and luscious dessert wine with the familiar muscat nose.	A	Spec

Wine	Colour	Country	Comments	Price	Avail
NÁGYBURGUNDI	R	*Hung.*	A fair stab at growing the temperamental Pinot Noir, soft and pleasant.	A	W/A
NAVARRA	R	*Sp.*	Increasingly good wines, the best are similar in style to woody Riojas.	A. B	W/A
NORMANNO	R. W	*It. Sicily*	Goodish whites and reds of consistent quality.	A	Spec
OREGON	R. W	*U.S.A.*	New style North American wines with a sharper edge due to a greater acidity.	A	W/A
ORVIETO		*It. Umbria*	Well known fullish dry whites, the Classicos which are still traditionally made are best.	B. C	Spec
OTHELLO	R	*Cyprus*	Bland factory-made red.	A	W/A
PASSE-TOUT-GRAINS		*Fr. Burgundy*	Seldom seen anachronism, a bland blend of two good grape types, Gamay and Pinot Noir.	B	Trad
PENEDÈS	R. W	*Sp.*	Recently arrived Spanish area thanks to skilled growers such as Torres and Leon.	A. D	W/A
PERIQUITA	R	*Port.*	Branded and blended plain red.	A	Trad
PETIT CHABLIS	W	*Fr. Burgundy*	Crisp fish wine, slight Chablis.	B. C	Trad
PINOT GRIGIO	W	*It.*	Widely grown and successful grape making fullish, rich whites.	A. B	Trad
PINOT GRIS	W	*Fr. It. Germ. Yugo. Aus.*	Flavoursome wines, French version of above.	A	Trad
PINOT NOIR	R	*Fr. Burgundy and elsewhere*	Thin, light reds normally stream from this reluctant traveller, except in the Côte d'Or where it occasionally achieves greatness.	A. D	W/A
PINOTAGE	R	*S.A.*	Rich, smooth, reliable reds of no great elegance or complexity.	B	W/A

Wine	Colour	Country	Comments	Price	Avail
PITSILIA	W	*Cyprus*	Pleasant white, grown in an area of impressive scenery.	A	Spec
PLAVAĆ MALI	R	*Yug.*	Indigenous red grape, making strong dark velvety wines. (See Dingac and Postup).	A	Spec
POMEROL	R	*Fr. Bordeaux*	Soft easy going value for money clarets, the best names age well. Petrus the rich trendies' favourite is ridiculously expensive.	A. D	W/A
PORT [DRY]	W	*Port.*	Virile, sunny and fortified aperitif, clumsier than good dry sherry.	C	W/A
PORTUGIESER	R	*Ger.*	Undernourished little picnic red.	A	Trad
POSTUP	R	*Yug. Dalmatia*	Mellow holiday red, dark and a little on the sweet side.	A	Spec
POUILLY FUMÉ	W	*Fr. Loire*	Sharp, tangy aperitifs, superb with fish.	B	W/A
POUILLY-FUISSÉ	W	*Fr. Burgundy*	Famous if, usually, fairly ordinary dry Chardonnays.	B	W/A
PRIMATICCIO	R	*It. Piedmont*	One of Italy's several attempts at a Beaujolais Nouveau type wine.	A	Spec
PROKUPAC	R	*Yug.*	Widely grown black grape yielding solid reds and rosés.	A	Spec
QUARTS DE CHAUME	W	*Fr. Loire*	Cool tartly sweet wine, especially when cellared a while.	D	Trad
QUINCY	W	*Fr. Loire*	Another crisp fish wine from the worthy Sauvignon Blanc.	B	W/A
RAMITELLO	W. R Spk	*It. Molise*	Good drinking wines, from a plain white to a quite respectable Chianti style red.	B	Spec

Wine	Colour	Country	Comments	Price	Avail
RAPITALÀ	W	*It.* *Sicily*	A fair dry white from an able producer Conte de la Gatinais.	B	Spec
RECIOTO	R. W	*It.* *Veneto*	An old fashioned method of adding riper grapes to a fermenting must. The resultant wines are often clumsy and headachy.		
REFOSCO	R	*It.* *Fruili-* *Venezia* *Giulia*	A happy little red veering from fizzy to fine.	A. C	W/A
RIESLANER	W	*Ger.*	Another sparsely grown perfumed vine with Riesling as a parent. The Rhinehessen examples are interesting.	B. C	Trad
RIESLING	W	*Ger.* *and* *elsewhere*	The best grape in the world for fruity, medium sweet wines. The finest examples are still made in the Rheingau.	A. D	W/A
RIOJA	R. W	*Sp.*	Previously a welcome oasis in a desert of very ordinary stuff, now heading a select group of emerging Spanish wines.	A	W/A
ROSSESE DI ALBENGA	R	*It.* *Liguria*	Variable red which legend has it was yet another favourite of Napoleon.	B. D	Spec
ROTGIPFLER	W	*Aus.*	Medium sweet to sweet whites of acceptable quality.	A	Trad
ROUCHET [ROCHÉ]	R	*It.* *Piedmont*	Interesting hilly red capable of developing well in bottle.	B	Spec
RUBESCO	R	*It.* *Umbria*	The riserva is among Italy's best reds.	B	W/A
RUEDA	Yel	*Sp.* *Old Castile*	Traditionally an oxidised white wine, a clean tasting modern version is also made.	B	Trad

Wine	Colour	Country	Comments	Price	Avail
SOAVE	W	*It.* *Veneto*	Tremendously popular and generally reliable white, but try a Classico Superior from a Bolla or Bertani.	A–B	W/A
SPÄTBUR-GUNDER	R	*Ger.*	Generally ignored light German reds of surprising style and potential.	B	Trad
SQUILLACE	W	*It.* *Calabria*	Flowery little thing, golden and quite delicious.	A. B	Spec
STEEN	W	*S.A.*	Scented but bland French transplant.	A	W/A
STERI	W. R	*It.* *Sicily*	Useful table wines thick reds and frisky whites.	A. B	Trad
SYRAH	R	*Fr.* *Rhône and elsewhere*	Big, soft and agreeable, even when young, they develop to some extent but these initially plump and pleasant wines seldom achieve real distinction.	A. D	W/A
SZAMORODNI	Oxid	*Hung.*	Hungarian for oxidised white wine.	B	W/A
SZÜRKEBARÁT	W	*Hung.*	Yet another name for the hard-working Pinot Gris, usually smooth party or picnic wines.	A	Trad
TAURASI	R	*It.* *Campania*	Goodish red for devotees of sunburnt Italian wines.	B. C	Spec
TAVEL	Rs	*Fr.* *Rhône*	Massive pink wine, despised by lovers of Mateus Rosé.	B	W/A
TERRE ROSSE	W	*It.* *Emilia-Romagna*	Vaunted Chardonnay from reputable grower.	C	Spec
TIGNANELLO	R	*It.* *Tuscany*	Brilliant Tuscan red with style and complexity.	D	Trad
TOCAI	W	*It.* *widely dispersed*	Pinot Gris again, quite successful all over Italy.	A. B	W/A

Wine	Colour	Country	Comments	Price	Avail
TOKAY	Amb	*Hung. Tokay*	Toffee flavour with sherry overtones, ranging from medium sweet to the sublime Eszencia.	B–D	Trad
TORRE DI GIANO	W	*It. Umbria*	Plodding white stablemate of Rubesco.	C	Spec
TRAMINER (TRAMINAC, GEWÜRZ-TRAMINER)		*Fr. Alsace, Ger. Sp. Yug. It. Calif. Ore*	Big flavoured, fleshy and fragrant, whites of generally reliable quality.	B–D	W/A
TROLLINGER	R	*Ger.*	Another esoteric pinky red but surprisingly tasty in the region of its birth.	B. C	Trad
VALBUENA	R	*Sp. Old Castile*	Excellent younger, if less brilliant versions of Vega Sicilia (Q.V.).	C. D	Spec
VACQUERYRAS	R	*Fr. Rhône*	Soft and sunny, reasonably priced reds of good quality.	B	W/A
VALPOLICELLA	R	*It. Veneto*	Luncheon wines traditionally but the Recioto version is heavy and strong.	A	W/A
VEGA SICILIA	R	*Sp. Old Castile*	A giant among wines, classic rich oaky red, a snip if compared to the best clarets.	D	Spec
VENEGAZZU	R	*It. Veneto*	The best Venetian red, leaning towards Bordeaux it is soft, lean, fine flavoured and consistently good.	B	Trad
CÔTES DU VENTOUX	R. W	*Rhône*	Strong, sound and unexciting.	A. B	Trad
SAINT-VÉRAN	W	*Fr. Burgundy*	Fruity dry Chardonnays of some quality and some depth.	B	W/A
VERDICCHIO	W	*It. Marches*	An established favourite, some modern versions are insipid. Bottles labelled Castelli di Jesi are above par.	A. B	W/A

Wine	Colour	Country	Comments	Price	Avail
VERÍN	R	*Sp. Galicia*	Strong and masculine reds.	B	Spec
VERDUZZO (RAMANDOLA)	W	*It. Fruili-Venezia Giulia*	Made to suit all tastes from crisp to sickly. Wines labelled Amabile are soft and fairly sweet.	B.C	Trad
VERDUZZO	W	*It. Fruili-Venezia Guilia*	Appetizing dry aperitifs.	A	Trad
VERMENTINO	W	*It. Sardinia*	A grape responsible for whites of varying sweetness, the Aragosta is recommended.	A. B	Spec
VERNACCIA DI ORISTANO	Amb	*It. Sardinia*	The best compares with the delicious Palo Cortado (Q.V.).	C. D	Spec
VERNACCIA DI SAN GIMIGNANO		*It. Tuscany*	As above and fresher cleaner versions too, also produced.	C. D	Spec
VIGNELAURE (CHÂTEAU)	R	*Fr. Provence*	"Whole" additive free fine wine with claret pretentions.	C. D	Trad
VIN DE CONSEIL	W	*It. Valle d'Aosta*	Smart, fresh dry wine made by a priest.	A. B	Spec
VIN JAUNE	Amb	*Fr. Jura*	Expensive and salty old relics, worth a try if one is rich and inquisitive.	D	Trad
VIN SANTO	Amb	*It. Trentino-Alto Adige*	Syrupy dessert wine, velvety stong and spicey.	C–D	Spec
VIÑA AND (GRAN) VIÑA SOL	W	*Sp. Penedès*	Solid if one dimensional whites from the excellent Torres stable.	B. C	W/A
VINHO VERDE	W. R	*Port. Minho*	"Green" wine can be white or red, usually lively thirst quenchers.	A	W/A
VINO NOBILE DI MONTELPUL-CIANO	R	*It. Tuscany*	Apart from having one of the longest names in Italy this is fine wine.	D	Trad

Wine	Colour	Country	Comments	Price	Avail
VINOT̀	R	*It.* *Piedmont*	Instant wine, quite good Nouveau from the powerhouse Nebbiolo grape.	A	Trad
VIOGNIER	W	*Fr.* *Rhône*	Expensive novelties from the northern end of the valley, superb when good but can also disappoint.	A	Trad
VOUVRAY	W	*Fr.* *Loire*	Good medium whites, growers say we drink them too dry in the U.K.	B	W/A
VRANAC	R	*Yug.*	Great inexpensive red, claret like, quite sophisticated and fine if cellared a while.	A	Spec
WEISSHERBST	Rs	*Ger.* *Baden*	Peculiar pink wine, can be very sweet.	A. D	Trad
YECLA	R. W	*Sp.* *Levant*	An emerging area using new methods to make quite acceptable wines.	A	Trad
ZIARFANDLER	W	*Aus.*	Standard hock style white, medium dry and versatile.	A	Trad
ZILAVKA	W	*Yug.*	Hard, oxidised, but eventually appealing wine once the taste is acquired.	A	W/A
ZINFANDEL	R	*Calif.*	Soft pungent red with limited improvement potential.	A. B	W/A
ZWEIGELT	R	*Aus.*	Interesting plummy thirst quencher from a native grape.	A	Spec

ACKNOWLEDGEMENTS

I wish to thank the following whose practical help was much appreciated; Antony Witherby whose guidance throughout the writing of the book was invaluable, his wife Brigid for her illustrations, James John M.W. and the Sociètè Civile de Château Latour, for helping to obtain, and permission to reproduce, a mint copy of their famous 1961 vintage label. Also I am indebted to those authors and experts whose writings proved such useful sources of reference: Jancis Robinson M.W., Serena Sutcliffe M.W., Hugh Johnson, Burton Anderson, Derek Cooper, Clive Coates M.W., Bill Warre M.W., Geoffrey Roberts, Robert M. Parker Junior, Mark Savage M.W., and the late André Simon and Professor George Saintsbury.

INDEX